DIGNITY

Acknowledgements

Discover Financial Services, Inc.
and Morgan Stanley
for your vision and enduring belief

Trevor
for your brilliant painting that captures
the essence of BOOST

Jerry
for your 11th hour support
that pushed the project over the top

Judy, Scott, and Susan
for your insight, creativity, technical expertise,
and gentle prodding

DIGNITY

12 EXTRAORDINARY INDIVIDUALS REACH FOR OPPORTUNITY

AS TOLD TO

DEBBIE & DALE INKLEY

SALT LAKE CITY

For information, contact
The Opportunity Foundation of America
2844 East Millcreek Canyon Road, P.O. Box 9748
Salt Lake City, UT 84109 USA
www.ofoa.net

Dignity: 12 extraordinary individuals reach for
    opportunity / as told to Debbie and Dale Inkley. -- 1st ed.
    p.   cm.
    LCCN: 2002113054
    ISBN: 0-9724692-2-2

    1. People with disabilities--Rehabilitation--Biography.
    2. People with disabilities--Services for. 3. People with
    disabilities--United States--Vocational guidance.
    4. BOOST (Salt Lake City, Utah) 5. People with
    disabilities--Attitudes. 6. Quality of life.
    I. Inkley, Debbie. II. Inkley, Dale.

    HV1552.3.D54 2003   362.4'048'0973
                                 QBI02-702004

Production Management by
Paros Press
1551 Larimer Street, Suite 1301
Denver, CO 80202
303-893-3332
www.parospress.com

BOOK DESIGN BY SCOTT JOHNSON

Printed in the United States of America
1   3   5   7   9   10   8   6   4   2

Contents

"*Character cannot be developed in ease and quiet. Only through experience of trial and suffering can the soul be strengthened, vision cleared, ambition inspired, and success achieved.*"

—Helen Keller

The Stories Begin...

The intrinsic value of the human soul is rooted in personal dignity, often described by words such as self-esteem or self-respect. The stories you will read in this book are true. They describe in intimate detail the daily battles waged by 12 individuals to maintain their self-respect, enhance their self-esteem, and internalize a new sense of personal dignity.

You will be inspired by their courage, amazed at their perseverance, and ultimately, grateful for their extraordinary example of achievement in the face of discouragement. However, the unselfish act of allowing us a glimpse into their private struggles has perhaps required even greater courage. These individuals have exposed their most tender vulnerabilities so that we might learn from their experience. We respect them for their triumph over adversity; we honor them for their willingness to share the events of their life in such a personal way.

The 12 stories are woven together with a common thread: a program called BOOST (Business Organization & Occupation Service Training). In 1994, a team of executives from Discover Financial Services, along with Debbie Inkley, set out to make a difference for people with physical, emotional, financial, and domestic challenges. They designed the BOOST program to provide real-life business experience, such as computer competence, problem-solving expertise, goal-setting skills, and, most importantly, a heightened sense of self-esteem – all at no cost to participants.

J. Nathan Hill, former president of Discover Bank and current Head of Operations, Consumer Banking Group International for Morgan Stanley, explains how he feels about BOOST: "An amazing transformation takes place in the inner and outer person of those who go through the BOOST Program and those of us who provide support. Participants enter the program financially, mentally, physically, or emotionally challenged with very little, or bruised self-esteem. They emerge eight weeks later with a revitalized spirit, a 'can do' attitude, enhanced self-image, and a 'toolbox' of skills – ready and wanting to take on the world! Those of us at Discover Financial Services and Morgan Stanley, who provide support, emerge better human beings because we have made a positive difference in the lives of other human beings. It's magic!"

BOOST is a straightforward, uncomplicated process that recognizes human values and potential. Participants gain marketable skills with a renewed sense of personal worth and self-confidence. Government and community agencies are more successful through cost-effective client training and job placement. Employers receive a pool of qualified prospective employees from a previously under-utilized human resource, and the company culture is dramatically influenced through sensitivity, awareness, mutual respect, and practical diversity.

The BOOST classroom is truly a microcosm of society. People come together from different backgrounds, with different challenges and abilities, and find that they are more alike than different. They bond quickly, supporting each other in unusual ways. One BOOST graduate says, "I came in as an individual, but I'm now part of a family." Another says, "I developed my own self-worth by learning how to give to others."

Such was the case in one of the Phoenix, Arizona classes. Anthony and Jose, two young-adult participants, were purposely seated on either side of Joanne, a 68-year-old grandmother with poor eyesight. Joanne had never touched a PC, whereas the young men were very proficient with their computer skills. Soon, Anthony and Jose became unofficial tutors for Joanne, while she became an example of quality life skills for them.

It was through casual conversation during the second week of class that Anthony and Jose discovered that Joanne was taking a long, multi-transfer bus ride to get to BOOST. The young men immediately offered Joanne a ride to and from class, a service they performed every day for the remaining six weeks until graduation. The chances are slim to none that Anthony and Jose would ever have met Joanne, let alone bond as friends; another example of the magic of BOOST.

The people who come to BOOST have a common goal of independence, respect, and gainful employment. Over 2,700 people have graduated from nine BOOST programs located in Sandy, Utah; West Valley City, Utah; Salt Lake City, Utah; Phoenix, Arizona; New Castle, Delaware; New Albany, Ohio; Riverwoods, Illinois; Chicago, Illinois; and Cumbernauld, Scotland.

While their lives are linked through the BOOST experience, each of the 2,700 graduates has a compelling personal story to tell. They have proven their ability in the face of disability, their hope in the face of misfortune, and their strength in the face of adversity.

The stories of the 12 extraordinary individuals we have included in this volume are representative of the immense challenges that have been overcome and the dignity with which each BOOST graduate has emerged.

DIGNITY

Darryl

"RUN"

My legs propel me

Wind rushing past

My body pumping fast

Ground zero flight

My eyes focused future

Blurred images form

My spirit freely soars

High velocity meditation

I run in my mind

I see the gift of it

You run in reality

You see only the act of it

— Darryl McQueen

1

*N*ow that boy is nuts," was the most often expressed opinion by those who were lucky enough to catch a glimpse of the young skateboarder. With both feet strategically placed on the board, Darryl used all of his strength to push off with one of his crutches as he began the thrilling descent to the bottom of the steep hill. His velocity accelerated to warp-skateboard speed before he confidently extended his arms, each holding a crutch for maximum balance and control. The feeling was unbelievable! Darryl was experiencing first-hand the exhilaration of the wind rushing past his face at breakneck speed, a sensation that had been stolen from him years earlier as the result of a debilitating disease called polio.

Darryl surely had a unique advantage over the other kids because he was able to balance his equilibrium by utilizing the wooden crutches that also served as his personal contact with mobility. No one seemed to mind the implied advantage. After all, when the ride was finished, Darryl had a far-greater challenge to use those same crutches to slowly make his way back up the hill for another try.

This was not the first hill Darryl McQueen had ever climbed. His life had been jammed full of hills and valleys, beginning with the first diagnosis of polio at age three and a half months. For the next 17 years, he was the only person to be stricken with polio in the entire state of Michigan. Then, in 1976, a little girl was unfortunately infected with the poliovirus. In the same spirit that has characterized his life, Darryl would have preferred to take that "honor" to his own grave.

There had been times, after he had grown old enough to understand, when Darryl wondered if God had purposely placed these barriers in his life as a test to see what he would do. Later, armed with even greater perspective, Darryl remembers, "I stopped feeling like I was picked on, that this kind of thinking was plain garbage. Hey! This is all I've ever known, so why feel like I was picked on?"

The son of a compassionate, loving mother and a self-educated father who came from serious poverty, Darryl was greatly influenced by the cultural input that was present in his young life. He and his eight siblings were encouraged to read, go to museums, and attend a wide variety of cultural events. Even though they lived in a tough neighborhood in Detroit, every child in the family attended college, a result of the prime value that his parents placed on education, hard work, and accountability. Brothers and sisters became CPA's, business professionals, air traffic controllers, and schoolteachers.

Darryl cannot talk about his life without talking about his mother. To him, she is the symbol of all that is good in the world. Her inner strength was the perfect complement for her sensitive, easy-going external nature. While very quiet, she was able to influence those around her in a powerful way. She knew how to love without condition, how to achieve without justification, and how to live without guile. She was an intelligent woman who worked hard for everything she had. Her wonderful example penetrated the soul of each of her children.

When she passed away, an uncomfortable feeling of melancholy settled upon Darryl. He became very sad as he contemplated the great loss he was required to endure. Somehow, in the depth of his advancing depression, he found the seed of his own creative expression. Feelings almost magically transformed into words as pen was put to paper and Darryl's poetry was born. Thoughts and images of his life are now permanently etched into a personal poetic picture of Darryl's world.

Memories like days on the football field as a young boy. Darryl learned how to prop himself up with his crutches to play defense. A fleet-footed ball carrier would be very surprised after running into the kid with the crutches who could knock people down with a solid tackle. Although he was quite small in stature, Darryl was very strong. His arms had held him up for most of his life so the well-developed upper body strength was a real advantage, especially when that was the only football-related asset he possessed. Mom was frequently upset about the broken crutches, the bruises, cuts, burns, broken bones, and other assorted injuries that accompanied Darryl's injury-prone and playful personality.

Frisbee, baseball, and dodge ball were also among the repertoire of sports that occupied the discretionary time of this adventuresome youth, all played with a distinct disadvantage produced by the poliovirus. In all of these activities, Darryl had definitely internalized the lessons he learned at his mother's feet. "She tried to make sure we understood that whatever the obstacle, you've just got to hang on," he warmly recalls. "She always said, 'If you can't say something good about somebody, don't say anything at all.' It may seem kind of corny if you think about it. To me, it means a lot more than the words say. It means that nothing that anybody can do or say about you can hurt you, so don't worry about it. Just try to say the positive thing and move on. If you can't deal with it, move on. That's how I've tried to live my life."

Personal disappointments began to appear with regularity. Darryl was not allowed to play on little league and school football teams, because crutches were illegal. Although it hurt not to be included, he took his mother's advice and moved on.

Darryl recognized at a very early age that he was different from his siblings.

"I always tell people that I started being a grown-up at three years old," he remembers. "We were moving and I was at the top of the stairs sitting on this dolly that I had to use while my back was still developing. All of my brothers and sisters were packing and moving and having a good time so I felt extremely separated. From that point on, I said 'Well, I must not be like the other little boys and if I'm not like the other little boys, then I am not a little boy anymore.' Even though I had certain childish things that I was doing, I really didn't feel very childish."

From kindergarten through ninth grade, Darryl attended a school for children with disabilities. His life was quite normal with laughing, kidding, practical jokes, and some trouble-making, probably much like other kids his age. He did feel the effects of being distanced from his family due to the philosophy, so prevalent at the time, of isolating people with disabilities. Darryl doesn't stay in close contact with his childhood friends from the school because of the pain of losing them. "To be in touch means you need to witness their deaths," he believes.

Graduation from a "regular" high school underscored some of what Darryl had always believed about himself. While most of the other graduates were announced with a list of clubs and achievements after their name, Darryl was a little embarrassed, even ashamed, when only his name was called. "But my mother seemed as proud of me as anybody," he remembers. "So as long as she is happy, I'll be happy."

Reflecting the strong work ethic that defined his family value system, Darryl was happy when he was working. Beginning at age 11, he worked in all kinds of jobs, from office work to gardener's assistant. On one occasion, a huge field was assigned to him to be hand-cut with a sickle in preparation for the lawn mower. It took about two months to complete the entire task. When finished, he would return to the other side of the field to start the process all over again. The patience Darryl learned from that experience has been utilized in many facets of his life.

Darryl was also hired to help a roofing contractor. His assignment was to dispose of old shingles that were removed from the houses. Hauling a 50-gallon barrel, weighing 250-300 pounds and filled with asphalt shingles, would be a formidable task for the strongest among us, . . . but a young man with polio? After filling the barrel with shingles, Darryl was responsible for dragging it to the dumpster for disposal. On one job, the dumpster was located on the other side of a fence without a gate. He would drag the barrel to the fence and then, with a giant heave, throw it over the barrier into the next yard. After lifting his body over the same fence, he would continue the journey to the distant dumpster.

Upper body strength was one of Darryl's biggest advantages during his youth. He was strong enough to climb the vertical rope at school by lifting himself hand over hand without using his legs. He had a muscular back in addition to powerful arms and great hand strength. Although his lower extremities were not very useful, Darryl's intense desire to remain active continued to supply the motivation for thoroughly experiencing his world.

Working with the City of Detroit as a fingerprint technician was one of Darryl's favorite jobs. He found the work fascinating. His training progressed rapidly. The more he learned, the more he enjoyed what he was doing. A career path began to emerge before Darryl, another dream that was dashed about 18 months later when budget shortfalls required a cutback in staff. Once again, the disappointment was demoralizing.

College became a focused objective as Darryl continued to search for meaningful job opportunities. Unfortunately, by his mid-twenties, he began to experience a significant loss of strength accompanied by an onslaught of intense knee and ankle pain. The pain in those powerful arms and shoulders even began to intensify. Today, Darryl is advised to avoid spending any time on his crutches even with the leg braces that are his constant companion. As he does with much of his life, Darryl waxes philosophical about his mode of mobile support. "Being in a chair does have its pluses," he suggests. "I can get places a lot quicker than I can on my crutches. But I can get more places on my crutches than I can in a wheelchair." Unfortunately, a less-than-perfectly-accessible world continues to limit his mobility.

Along with many of his disabled childhood friends, Darryl grew up knowing that the stares and ogling were part of his life. An inquisitive gaze from a curious child has never offended him. On the contrary, he has developed an engaging, charismatic personality that attracts far more than it repels. His keen sense of humor triggers a hearty laugh from his mellow deep voice that has an uncommon resemblance to Santa Claus. Even though he has always considered himself to be pretty shy, Darryl has put all who approach him at ease with his wonderful aura of warmth.

Children are special beneficiaries of his gentle nature. "If a child has a question . . . what bothers me is when parents say, 'Don't do that,'" he counsels. "Because I don't mind kids; actually kids accept me quicker than anything. They will be freaked out for a second until they find out what the deal is. When they stop staring and asking questions, now that's when I get concerned."

As a young adult living in Ohio, Darryl once again encountered the underbelly of life. He was engulfed by extreme depression, probably provoked by a skyrocketing blood sugar that measured the seriousness of his diabetic condition. He was unhappy and lonely. In the midst of this daily battle with depression, Darryl became the target of the Aryan Nations that was headquartered in his town.

They had been sending him disgusting hate mail for some time. "One day I came home and they had written the 'N' word all over my front door," Darryl remembers. He was frightened as well as angered by the public display of bigotry and prejudice. A group of these misguided troublemakers personalized the attacks against Darryl even more by standing at his window and yelling racial slurs and epitaphs in the middle of the night. He was proud of his African-American heritage. He couldn't understand what had precipitated this crazy vendetta against him. It's a question that still pleads for an answer.

At that time, Darryl had been in Ohio for almost 13 years. He had originally come to attend college in an effort to improve his chances of finding a quality job. "I'm going to take my shot at something," was his personal rallying cry. Now, after all those years laced with barriers and disappointments, he could almost see the end of the tunnel, a view that was substantially blurred by the depression that was nagging him.

A very delicate phase of life had been entered, one that was soon to prove more fragile than he had ever expected. Darryl was searching for something to hang onto while surrounded by intense bigotry, out of control diabetes, the advancing effects of polio, and the increasing bouts with depression. In a moment of extreme emotional trauma, he purposely ingested over 200 pills in a conscious effort to put his life in jeopardy. "But it was like there was this little voice telling me, 'Don't do it,'" Darryl recalls.

Responding to the internal message may have been one of

Darryl's finest hours; it undoubtedly required reaching into a dried-up emotional reservoir to find one last morsel of strength. He called somebody immediately after taking the pills and was rushed to the hospital, where his life was saved. While lying in the hospital bed, Darryl remembers contemplating the disturbing events that had combined so negatively to create the scenario. "There has got to be something out there," he thought.

Some positive events coalesced during a Christmas visit in Delaware. A caring sister introduced Darryl to a school friend who worked at Discover Card. Darryl returned to Ohio with the name and phone number of the BOOST Coordinator. After the holidays, he made a long-distance call to Delaware to investigate the opportunities that BOOST offered. He was encouraged in his desire to enter the program. "I know she didn't believe that I was actually going to go through with it and move to Delaware," Darryl recalls. "But I said, 'Give me a chance and I'm going to take care of it.'"

Latching onto BOOST was no small endeavor for Darryl. He made the move from Ohio to Delaware just to enter the program. He was given the same challenge as the other participants: "We're going to keep a commitment to you and make sure you get the training you need, if you will make a commitment to us to be here every day. That's all you need to do." The challenge took root with Darryl. Attending class every day to learn everything he could became his major focus.

Darryl quickly moved from a feeling of isolation and depression to a sense of being appreciated and respected. He became very popular with his BOOST classmates and Discover Card employees as his charismatic personality blossomed in the work environment. "You actually feel you can accomplish something," Darryl believes. "It's extremely meaningful. I didn't see people looking or staring; I just got a kick out of that. So, it relaxes you enough to where you feel that you can accomplish something without having to second-guess yourself and you can just go ahead and do it."

During this time, Darryl attracted opportunities like a magnet, a distinction that had been most recently reserved for problems. He was offered three jobs with different employers during his 10-week BOOST training, but he wanted to finish the program and work at Discover Card, a goal that was soon accomplished. "I am a customer service representative," Darryl proudly announces. "I answer the phone and, if you have any problems, hopefully I can help you. I like being able to correct people's problems, even though they call in and are all irate. I think I'm pretty good at getting them to calm down and relax. Most of the time they do have legitimate concerns."

Darryl credits the influence of his mother as the architect of his customer-centered empathy. "She was one of those people who never turns you down," he carefully articulates. "I don't know if I can ever get to the point where she was. I do strive to emulate her example."

As we all do, Darryl continues to struggle with the challenges of life. He considers the deteriorating strength in his legs to be a major issue along with his increased weight. He understands, however, that both positives and negatives are inherent in any situation. "Keep a good attitude and life will become what you want it to be," is Darryl's philosophy.

He has also developed a simple pair of guidelines for living. "Number one, know who you are," he says, "And second, don't run away from people who are trying to help you." He also has some good counsel in dealing with people with disabilities. "Ask the questions," he advises. "Whatever questions you have, don't keep them to yourself because that's just going to make you think that this person is different and can't be approached. Be like a kid and ask the questions."

Philosophy flows easily from Darryl's mellow bass voice. His advice grows even more potent as deep, resonant tones combine to reinforce the simple message. While his broadcast-quality voice has the potential to engulf a listener, Darryl's naturally shy nature and warm, caring personality create a moderating effect that soothes and reassures. At precisely the right moment, an infectious smile flashes across his face. Eyes twinkle mischievously as a deep, irresistible belly laugh completes the seduction. Few could ever resist falling prey to such a charismatic interchange.

Darryl uses his gift carefully to lift and encourage those around him. His unconditional love is available to all. Most embrace the opportunity to be touched by the wonderful blessing of Darryl's friendship, but his popularity has little to do with personal ego and everything to do with reaching out to brighten the lives of others. Such was the case at the BOOST reunion.

An excited buzz of anticipation drifted through the audience as Darryl maneuvered his wheelchair into position near the front row of chairs. With a coordinated thrust from those muscular arms, he strained to lift his body to an upright position. Braces that supported his legs and crutches that stabilized his balance were indispensable tools to enable Darryl during his impending journey to the microphone.

The room grew quiet. As one foot was placed ahead of the other, beads of perspiration began to appear on Darryl's forehead. His left foot slowly replaced his right in the lead position and the cycle continued to repeat itself until he triumphantly arrived at the podium a few steps away. He stretched his arms wide in celebration. The gigantic smile on his face electrified his cheering peers. No soaring eagle had ever accomplished a more amazing feat.

Darryl continues to visualize the gift of mobility only in his mind. But for this one courageous moment, he experienced the glorious reality of the act. Now, his spirit soars freely into the future, lifting all who are fortunate enough to be touched by his indomitable soul.

Debbie

※ ·❖·❖·◐◯◑·❖·❖· ※

The ball was placed perfectly over the plate. A big swing now would certainly result in a base hit. Debbie Tunstall was poised and ready. Knees bent. Arms flexed. Eye on the ball. All she needed was to connect with that fat pitch and she would prove once and for all that she wasn't such a klutz. With a mighty heave, her arms moved the bat in a level arc until the ball was engaged. The ball exploded off the bat when contact was made and flew high and deep to left center field. The outfielders had no chance to get there in time as the ball dropped into the gap between them.

Debbie had a chance for her first hit. It was never a problem of connecting with the ball; she had plenty of natural ability and coordination for that. Her problem was that now she had to run the bases. With all the energy she could muster, Debbie began the long trek to first base. Most people think a run of that length is no big deal, but for Debbie Tunstall it is an insurmountable obstacle. And on this day, history repeated itself. The ball arrived once again before she did and the fateful words, "You're out!" echoed in her mind.

Debbie knows how it feels to be "out." The seventh of eight children, she was regularly sick as a child. At six months her tonsils became so swollen and infected that she was described as clinically dead. Even after revival the problems continued with a serious reaction to the penicillin. She was almost lost again. Later, after her mother discovered a dip in her back, Debbie was casually diagnosed with an upside down hipbone.

Those early years were awfully difficult, but they were just the beginning. Debbie was quiet and short in stature compared to her siblings. Due to her constant sickness, she rapidly drifted into the background and became known as a major klutz. People constantly made fun of her because she couldn't run. The big elementary school race was humiliating. Debbie came in dead last, not only in the fifth grade, but also in the entire school. Fat kids beat her; short kids beat her; younger kids beat her; everyone beat her.

The upside down hipbone is what was suspected to be the root of the problem. However, at age 15, the diagnosis was changed to spinabifida. Debbie would literally pass out when she rose to her feet. After a series of tests and examinations by an army of doctors, the determination was made that her spinal cord was tethered at the bottom of her spine rather than a normal two-thirds of the way down. Each time she stood up, the cord would stretch and tear, causing her to faint from the pain and trauma. At the end of a typical day, her father would literally pick her up and carry her to bed because the pain of moving was so extreme. Major back surgery was the recommended remedy.

The year prior to her surgery, when Debbie was 14, her family moved to the little town of Albion, Idaho with a population of 350. It is nestled in a beautiful valley surrounded by hills and mountains that create a natural secure feeling. Debbie felt content in this wonderful little place, although she was continually sick and in pain. She carried pillows to school and received special consideration from her teachers because moving between classes often took 15 minutes rather than the allotted four. Her classmates were kind to her but her self-image continued to plummet.

The first of four surgeries during high school was performed in Salt Lake City, a four-hour drive from her home. She was in the hospital a week and in bed at home for another few weeks before returning to school. Her parents were greatly concerned about her welfare. They would have done anything possible to help relieve her suffering, but the diagnosis and ultimate operation had confirmed her father's greatest fear: His daughter was disabled. Debbie's sister was six foot one and the star of the basketball team. She was someone her father could take pride in and brag about. Before the surgery, Debbie was just uncoordinated, but now she was disabled. How do you brag about someone who is disabled? Besides, he felt responsible for her condition. Debbie could never understand why.

Not only was there a continual effort by her mother to apologize for what had happened, Debbie also felt a growing communication void with her parents. "I am really alright," Debbie would say, but she felt like they were somehow ashamed of her.

She knew her parents loved her. That was never a question. The distance between them grew, however, because of the vicious cycle that was created. Debbie blamed herself for her parents' bad feelings; she believed they were ashamed of her. Her parents, on the other hand, felt bad because of Debbie's condition and experienced their own feelings of guilt. The gap continued to widen when Debbie's singing talent was not recognized on the same level as the athletic abilities of her sisters. "How can you brag about a singer?" her father would ask, even though Debbie's singing performances were in high demand. While others were validating her, a sense of hopelessness was germinating because she felt like she was defective in her father's eyes.

As her self-esteem dropped, so did the quality and quantity of her relationships. She often had roller-coaster friendships with siblings and friends at school. People alternated between her best friends and worst enemies. Debbie felt like an outcast both at home and at school. "Feeling like an outcast is the loneliest feeling in the world," she explains. "You just don't want to wake up in the morning. I would find places to hide; places where I could just go and sit and be my own self and think and plan and dream."

Most people were uncomfortable being around Debbie. Each time she found someone who seemed to accept her for who she was, something would happen to alter the equation. She was often hurt by snide comments uttered behind her back. At times, she was the brunt of mean-spirited ribbing or unflattering jokes. The constant barrage of negative input became too great a burden. It was much easier to just be a loner, to escape into a private world unencumbered by people.

In addition to back problems caused by her tethered spinal cord, Debbie was also suffering from a serious urinary tract condition. Several surgeries were needed during her high school years to correct the problem. In retrospect, some of the surgical procedures probably contributed to the devastating kidney problems Debbie would encounter later in life. Many of the kids seemed to like her but they avoided her because she was fragile. They were probably just guilty of not knowing what to say and what to do.

Missing almost a year and a half of high school contributed to the alienation that Debbie felt. She cried constantly because she considered herself to be overweight and ugly, along with other physical challenges. She hated herself; she couldn't understand why God had given her so many obstacles to conquer. Her mother became impatient and frustrated. Her father continued to want her to achieve more than she thought she could. Though Debbie graduated with a B average, her academic achievement didn't measure up to her sister, who was class valedictorian. It didn't ever seem to be enough!

Following her high school graduation, a job in Twin Falls, Idaho became an important high-water mark in Debbie's life. She met warm, caring friends who accepted her without judgment. They had some wonderful times together, chock-full of fun and happiness. Her future husband was one of those she met. They developed a warm, platonic relationship and regularly "hung out" together at the same time he was dating other women. Then one day he realized that his best friend was a female. She had fallen for him earlier because he actually enjoyed her sense of humor. He found her jokes to be funny, her wit clever. No one had ever laughed at her jokes before. The more he laughed, the more she opened up. The more she opened up, the more people seemed to enjoy her. Finally, Debbie began to realize that she not only had a sense of humor but also a keen intellect.

Her boyfriend was 33 and she was 19, though most people thought she was older than he. All of the health and life challenges that Debbie had experienced helped to strengthen her. She was quiet and organized; he was a free spirit. A proposal of marriage followed a quick romance of just three or four months. He was ready for marriage; she knew she wasn't. Nonetheless, they were soon husband and wife.

Debbie was told that she would never have children because of the spinabifida. She and her husband were both quite shocked when she got pregnant shortly after their marriage. It was a bitter-sweet experience. Though they both wanted to have children, neither had a job. The pregnancy proved to be damaging to Debbie's future health. Symptoms began at about five months when she started blacking out. She fainted numerous times, often hitting her head when she fell. Doctors discovered she had toxemia and induced the baby when Debbie experienced temporary kidney failure.

Her kidney function returned quickly after the baby was born. Nevertheless, the decision was made to wait before having more children. Discovering numerous birth control methods that don't work led to two more children, each a year apart. The children were a joy for the family but they ultimately exacted an extremely high price: permanent kidney failure.

For many years, competent medical evaluation revealed no long-term problem. Positive results on her blood work didn't match the symptoms. Debbie's health was still very poor from the cumulative effects of her prior challenges, but she knew that something else was terribly wrong. During a period of three years, she had five broken legs, probably due to osteoporosis (a lack of calcium in the bones). One leg snapped just walking to church. After she dropped from normal status to 10 percent kidney function in less than one month, the correct diagnosis was finally made.

Debbie's weight ballooned to 320 pounds, a result of her countless health problems. She hated herself. Her husband believed there was nothing wrong with her. His reinforcement turned negative and abusive. He thought Debbie was lazy. He began to call her names, regularly making fun of her weight. She continued to hold her family together but not herself. Persistent kidney infections created the need for several foot amputation procedures. She lost a large amount of both feet a little at a time. There was no warning. A simple pinprick in a toe would soon mean the toe needed to be removed. When she lost the majority of her right foot, she also lost her job because she could no longer walk.

Her volatile marriage became too much to sustain so Debbie filed for divorce and took the kids. She had no job and no marketable skills, but she did have an unconquerable spirit and the responsibility of three children, all under 13. Vocational Rehabilitation helped her get back into college, where she began to feel better about herself. She and the children were living in a tiny apartment while Debbie was realizing, for the first time, that she was smart. Her grades reflected her intelligence. She gained confidence. Her commitment to the children was also strengthened; regardless of what happened to her, the kids had to come first in her life.

The kidney disease diagnosis occurred while she and her husband were separated. It jolted both of them, but he was especially hit hard. Her husband realized that he had been wrong to judge her so harshly. He also realized that they didn't have much time left to be together. He became a supportive husband, a responsible father, and, once again, Debbie's best friend.

Debbie, on the other hand, was living a recurring nightmare. "Why, God? Haven't I been through enough?" she asked herself. "Of all the things I have been through, why this? Why now? I have got to have time to raise my kids." The only solution was a kidney transplant. Without it, Debbie would not survive. Because of a rare blood type and the way her blood had changed through numerous bouts with toxemia, a matching kidney was a long shot, at best. No one in her family was a match. The average wait for a kidney transplant is three years. The projected waiting time for Debbie was 14 years, if ever.

Dialysis was immediately ordered. She could not sustain her life without it. Three sessions of four hours each per week became the designated schedule, plus travel and preparation time. Debbie considered her dialysis a part-time job. This was no ordinary job, however. It was an absolute requirement to live. There were ongoing downsides to the treatment. In one year alone, Debbie needed 13 surgeries to replace grafts in her arm for the dialysis needles.

Finally, a bold procedure was performed to install a catheter in her chest that goes directly into her heart. Never being one to fit the mold, Debbie doesn't seem to respond the way that other people would to considerable pain. An improper dose of medication almost cost her life and required an emergency transfusion. On several other occasions, she has gone into shock that required emergency procedures to stabilize her.

Very little about Debbie's health is typical, but she and her family do everything they can to make their life normal. The children regularly hear, "Oh, your mom is so incredible." Their response is typically, "My mom?" There is significant denial about mom's health in the safe place the children have found for themselves. They won't admit the problem is serious, and that is just what Debbie wants. In a moment of teenage frustration and argument, her daughter said, "Well, you don't have a mother who is dying." Debbie's response was simply, "Neither do you." Reality, at the time, supported her daughter's conclusion.

In the middle of the emotional roller-coaster ride through health issues, pain, separation, life-threatening diagnosis, reconciliation, and time-consuming treatment, practical material needs continued to compete for space in Debbie's life. She needed to find work. Because of her dialysis, most jobs were not adaptable to the necessary schedule. After exhausting other possibilities, her vocational rehabilitation counselor suggested that Debbie inquire about the BOOST program facilitated at Discover Card. Productive employment did not appear to be a realistic goal for Debbie but she knew she had to continue to try. Her call was rewarded.

"The BOOST program showed me some possibilities and I got really excited," Debbie says. "When I got into the program I was thrilled." David Salazar, the BOOST coordinator, helped her to identify things she hadn't really considered before. "He taught us that we had hidden abilities and talents we didn't recognize. He worked with us. He encouraged us. He loved us unconditionally." After all the disappointments, so many things that were taken away from her a piece at a time, Debbie began to see hope where she had only struggled for survival. Her legs were deformed from all the breaks. She had lost most of both feet. She was in constant pain. Her kidneys were non-functional. She needed dialysis just to stay alive. So many pieces had been lost; she didn't realize she had anything left.

Debbie successfully completed the BOOST program, where she gained acceptance, confidence, and new job skills. She learned that she had the ability to succeed in the competitive employment arena and was rewarded with a job at Discover Card. She felt much better about herself. A lifetime of eroding self-esteem had been replaced with an assurance that she could succeed. "I am happier now than I have been in my entire life," Debbie says, "and part of that has been the kidney failure. I know it sounds weird, but the kidney failure taught me that most things I thought were important really aren't. I am able to toss the junk aside and concentrate on what really matters."

She is still confronted with constant challenges but Debbie Tunstall knows that she is not "kidney failure." A disability is a backpack to carry; it is not the whole person. She doesn't want to just be alive, she wants to have a life, however short that might be. There is too much to do, too much to learn, too much to accomplish to worry about how long life will be. While depression is a constant battle, she won't allow it to control her. Not long ago, she got blood poisoning from a hole in her catheter. A friend at work rushed her to the hospital, where she was stabilized. The doctor told her she only had about a half hour to make the trip. She would have died had it taken any longer. After a week in the hospital, almost half in ICU, and three days at home, Debbie was back at work because she doesn't have time to stay in bed. After this serious episode, her daughter told her, "Mom, if you weren't dying so often, we would care more."

Kidney failure, infection, poisoning, and pain are not the focus of Debbie's life. The true focus is Jared's choir concert, Jennifer's volleyball game, her husband, and her job. Debbie enjoys the tiny pleasures like sitting in the sun on the grass or the smell of the rain. She knows she is special, but believes that everyone is. "I have so much fun finding the special in people. That is really the joy of life, though, isn't it?" Debbie asks. "When we look at people and pity or feel badly for them, we miss out on all the goodness and all the depth and ability they have when we concentrate on the disability."

What does the future hold for Debbie Tunstall? "I don't honestly know," she says. "I could be dead tomorrow. I don't care. What is important is that I am doing the best I can with the days that I have, that I am having the opportunity to love my children so that when I am not here they know they were loved. I don't know how much time I've got, but while I'm here I have the opportunity to learn and grow. I don't want to waste a minute of that precious time."

Debbie no longer feels sorry for herself. She doesn't ask "Why me?" Her constant query is, "What can I do to help someone else?" She looks past unbelievable barriers to find possibilities and she looks for the best in others. "The only people that I feel sorry for are the people who feel sorry for themselves," is Debbie's philosophy. "They are missing out and it's their own fault. I don't care how sick you are. There is something you can do, there is something you can learn, there is some way you can grow."

Another ball is headed for the outfield. This time it clears the fence for a towering home run. Debbie has kept her eye on the ball. She won't be called out at first or second or third. She will cross home plate, regardless of how long it takes to circle the bases, with her head held high, a smile on her face, and her arms held triumphantly in the air. We all cheer for her because she is no longer "out." A short time ago Debbie Tunstall received a new kidney. She is finally "safe," at last.

David

—————✦━◆━◗◯◖━◆━✦—————

The word around Judge Memorial High School was that
David Salazar had all the connections. He could get
you anything you wanted at any time. If you had your
eye on a new stereo for your car, "Mr. Connections" could get it for
29 bucks. If you needed some lunch tickets, he could deliver for
half price. Chico, as David was known, had tried to earn the
respect of his classmates by building a reputation founded on mis-
direction. Anyone could buy a Graco stereo for $29, and the lunch
tickets came from David's own discount purchases because of his
family's financial situation.

It was part of a concerted effort that David used to gain
popularity while masking the lifelong secret that continued to stalk

him. The mask he had constructed began to take on even more aggressive proportions as David found that he could protect himself from ridicule by striking first. "People were guilty until proven innocent," was David's motto. "I figured that if they knew I would do anything in my power to hurt them first, they wouldn't try to hurt me."

What was the genesis of this hostility, the secret that David had worked so hard to protect since childhood? The answer is found in a note that David wrote in the sixth grade, about the time he realized there was something different about him. "Dear God, why did you make me like this? I'm just a little boy. I just want to talk and play like everyone else. I can sing, I can walk, I can even run. Why do all the problems start when I try to talk?" It was a little prayer that David had written, one that he has in his possession to this day. "I was hoping that God would make me stop stuttering," David remembers.

The Salazar family was deeply religious and very close. "Family was what life was all about," David says. "It wasn't about money; it was always about family and helping people." The son of a Mexican immigrant mother and a father who was born in the state of New Mexico, David was the last of six children. "We spoke Spanish at home and we spoke English outside of the home," David recalls. "We were always taught to speak English when there were other people present who didn't understand Spanish." The bilingual training of his early life actually proved very helpful as David became proficient in both languages and learned to speak

"Spanglish" to cover his stutter. "What I couldn't say in Spanish I'd say in English, and when I couldn't say something in English, I'd switch to Spanish. It worked very well for me."

David and his childhood friends paid little attention to his different speech patterns until the sixth grade. "I remember it perfectly," David says. "The first day of school, I remember getting to my name and I couldn't spit it out. All of my friends looked at me like 'What's wrong with David?' We had all grown during the summer and when we came back it was no longer David, it was David the Stutterer – maybe not in their eyes, but I finally noticed I was different."

As the realization began to unfold, David thought it was his fault that he had this stutter, that he was doing something wrong. "Every New Year's I made a promise that I would never stutter again," he recalls. David's father sat down with him to share the history of his own challenge with stuttering. "And to tell you honestly," David shares, "What he said meant nothing to me at the time. He told me he loved me and I thought he was just trying to make me feel good."

A family visit with his great aunt a couple of years later helped David understand the depth of his father's compassion. "My dad always being the trickster he was, walked over to this little Mexican lady, probably four foot nothing, tried to hug her and purposely missed her. He looked down and said, 'Oh, there you are.' The aunt playfully said, 'Oh there's my A A A A A A A Antonio.' I asked another aunt, 'Why did aunty do that to him?' She said, 'Your dad used to stutter and couldn't say his name.'"

This revelation was very powerful for David. It was his first real indication that he was not alone, that his father did understand the frustrating experience of talking through a stutter. He could really appreciate the frustration of picturing the things he wanted to say in his mind, but somehow certain words got blocked, especially his own name. He did understand how trying harder made it even more difficult to express himself. But most importantly, his father had conquered it. David finally saw some light at the end of the tunnel.

The first days of a new school year were some of the most challenging for David during his junior high experience. He was frightened to speak in public, a surefire exposure of his secret. Each of the class members would take a turn reading. David was more preoccupied with finding his place in the rotation than listening to what the others were reading. He remembers, "My heart was beating out of my body. I was scared to say my own name." Perhaps, it was under that intense pressure that David learned he could alter his language, and even his name, to avoid the stutter that caused him so much fear. It also proved to be the headwaters of his anger that later overflowed from the mask he was creating.

By high school, a stark contradiction had developed between the self-image that David carried and his parents' commitment to provide a quality education for their two sons, David and his older brother, Felix. Their parents worked tirelessly and went without a lot of material things in order to send the boys to private Catholic schools.

Felix, always one of David's heroes, has waged a life-long

battle with tourette syndrome. He worked hard in school but was mistreated by many of his classmates. David, on the other hand, became very popular in high school. His popularity, however, was in direct contrast to his scholastic achievement. "I felt really dumb and stupid," David says. "I felt like I couldn't learn anything." For David, school wasn't at all about education, it was a social thing. "It was about how to get people to like me or keep them from hurting me," David remembers.

He loved basketball but wasn't able to call the plays, a major responsibility of the point guard position David so desperately wanted. Obstacles and frustration seemed to dog him in every phase of his life. His family was always very compassionate and understanding. David's home became a safe haven as he continued to wrestle with a communication style that would shield him from the ridicule of his peers. He became very self-conscious of his stutter. Age and physical maturity did not mellow his frustration. On the contrary, he became more angry and aggressive, always looking to prove himself by picking a fight every chance he got.

In the classroom, David performed at the level of his self-image, carrying a grade point average of 2.1, just high enough to graduate from high school. His anger began to manifest in his social life. The natural evolution of David's defense mechanism was to become mean, disrespectful, and rude. He would do anything necessary to deflect attention from his speech disorder. That is where the nickname, Chico, came from. It was one of the only names that David could spout on cue, so he decided to call himself

Chico. Many of his high school and post high school friends still call him Chico to this day.

After graduation from Judge Memorial, David was confronted with some sobering decisions about his life. He decided to attend the University of Utah, but had no idea what he wanted to do. "I was really scared," David painfully recalls, "I knew nothing about what I was going to face in college." Since his "Mr. Connections" gig had proven so successful in high school, David decided to find his niche at the U. "Like an idiot, I went in there trying to do the same thing I did at Judge," he laments. "I learned how to make ID's and everyone, including the whole football team, came to me wanting a fake ID." Finding himself in unknown territory and on the edge of something sinister, David asked himself, "What am I doing? This isn't part of the plan. You don't do this." The mask was becoming more well-defined and Chico decided to stop his rather lucrative side job.

The next hurdle in college was even more difficult. David chose general education classes during that first quarter. They were very large and didn't require much class participation. Most of them, however, did have a policy to call the roll out loud and those in attendance needed to say "here" to be counted present. David was not comfortable with the public verbal response, so most of the time he just remained silent. While he attended almost all of the classes, he was not counted as being present more than 25% of the time. Nor did he participate in the oral presentations that were a large part of his grade. The result was a dismal GPA of 1.2 on the 4.0 scale.

Subsequent quarters that first year saw a continuing decline in both David's interest and attendance. He refused to talk or ask questions. He adopted the philosophy of "Shut up and nobody will know," until one day he was asked a direct question by a professor. All his experience at masking the stutter failed him as he tried to form the words to answer the question. The more he pressed, the more he stuttered until all the students, and the professor, were laughing hysterically at him. David quietly picked up his books and left the room, making a decision to totally withdraw from school. An external force, once again, stripped the mask silently away.

That night, in response to his disillusionment with school, David went out drinking. He explains, "I came home late just bombed out of my mind and my mom and everyone was saying, 'What's wrong with you?'" David had not been totally honest with his family about his negative and somewhat sporadic experience during that first year of college. In fact, he didn't bother to tell his parents that he had withdrawn from all of his classes in the third quarter and wasn't going to school at all.

A job at an automotive paint supply store became the focus of David's career after the frustrating experience with that first year of college. He was not required to talk at the store. He worked hard, became very proficient at his job, and was promoted to be an important member of the staff. His simmering anger would easily boil over when he went to a bar and had a few drinks. He was constantly looking for fights, not necessarily even needing a reason. "I was hanging out with the wrong crowd," David admits. "But during that time I knew I wasn't really happy, 'cuz I wasn't living the life that I wanted."

He met a girl, nurtured the relationship, and bought an engagement ring to give to her. Then, within the space of one week, he found that his potential fiancée was cheating on him, the store he worked in accused him of stealing (a mistake they made that was later retracted), and his new truck was burglarized with everything inside stolen. David had succeeded in rebuilding portions of his mask with two bases of security: his girlfriend and his job. She talked for him, did everything for him. His job was the financial security that provided material resources to buy his new truck and "be somebody." Now, both of those supports had collapsed and he felt once again like an open wound.

David was beside himself. He wanted to lash out at anyone who had caused him pain. He found out who had come between him and his girlfriend and drove to the house, armed with a baseball bat with nails driven into it. David recalls the experience with a great deal of relief. "I waited until 4:00 a.m. and the guy finally showed up. I got out of the truck with my baseball bat and the guy started to cross the road. Voices are talking to me, my mom, my dad, everybody. 'Hey! Don't be so stupid, don't be dumb!' I turned around, got back into my truck, went home and spilled my guts."

That night, David shared his most intimate feelings with his parents. He told them he had lost his job the previous week and had not been going to work. He told them what his girlfriend, who had been informally adopted into the Salazar family, had done. His mom comforted David by telling him, "No one has ever died of a broken heart; there's always some way to mend."

His father told David that he hated to see what his son was going through, that he understood his pain. David's response was defensive, "Dad, you don't know what it's like; you have no idea what it's like." Then, in a very special teaching moment, Antonio Salazar, the ever wise and patient father, shared the details of a hushed story from his own life that helped David understand that his father really did understand the pain he was suffering. "He was really teaching me a lot and I was starting to listen to what he was saying," David remembers.

Somewhere the spark of a better life flickered inside of David. He was introduced to a group called NSP (National Stutter-ing Project). It wasn't exactly David's style for dealing with his speech disorder, but he did begin the process of reaching out for help. He got a job in a grocery store as a night stocker and by David's own description, "partied pretty hard five days a week for almost a year." Not being particularly enamored of his grocery store job, David made the decision to apply at the Discover Card Operations Center, a move that conjures up strange images for most of us. What would possibly possess a person like David, after spending a lifetime trying to escape involvement in public dis-course, to go to a place where you had to talk on the telephone for a living? His response is brusque and succinct, "Because I was sick and tired of people telling me that I couldn't do it."

The decision was incredibly courageous and demonstrates a new technique in David's attempt to fashion the perfect mask by stripping it all away. But it was very difficult for him. "Oh, man! I never was so scared," David remembers. "I felt so stupid because one day in my training I stood up and told everybody, 'You know I've got this stuttering thing and I don't want you to feel uncomfortable.'" That was the first time in his life that David had ever done anything like that. There were many times that he wanted to quit because he would often stutter on every syllable during mock training conversations. A patient training staff and a terrific group of people in his training class gave David constant encouragement and reinforced his self-esteem.

The result of the "hard partying" that continued for a time after his hiring at Discover Card yielded a different result. "I found myself an angel, my wife, Jennifer," David proudly asserts. "I saw her in a bar, of all places. I never thought I would meet somebody like her." The pickup line that David used was not exactly the most polished or suave, but it seemed to work. "Didn't you used to ride the bus to Judge Memorial?" he asked Jennifer. Her affirmative answer was the beginning of a courtship that blossomed into marriage vows.

David was very good at hiding his stutter from women on dates. "I'd order things I didn't like or want so I didn't have to say words I couldn't say," David laughs. "I even called myself by dozens of different names. I'd lie or say anything I needed to say to avoid stuttering." But Jen was different! David couldn't hide his stutter from her because it simply didn't matter to Jen. She saw in David an intelligent, caring, good man, a person of great worth. Together they set out to practically apply the values that David had learned from his parents.

Education, of course, was right at the top of the list. Since David had performed so dismally during his first year at the University of Utah, he couldn't get back into school as a full-time student without special approval, appearance before a review board, and two probationary quarters of 3.0 grades or above to prove himself. He was also required to take some difficult classes as part of the probation. With the help of Jen and others, David completed his trial period and was granted full-time student status. He took some speech therapy classes and his first question was, "Do you think I could become a speech therapist?" The answer was a resounding "No!" He was told that he wouldn't be good at helping people because he stuttered. David proved them wrong. He graduated from the University of Utah with a major in Communication Disorders and a GPA of 3.4. "Speech therapy helped me," David confirms, "but it all started when Jennifer helped me see that I was a truly good man; that I never was this bad person, this mean person, this jerk."

Jennifer Salazar is a Special Education teacher for hearing-impaired children. She understands the value of a high level of self-esteem for children with disabilities. Indeed, David believes Jen was instrumental in helping him develop a sense of worth that has carried him through some difficult times. "She helped me value myself and understand who I was. And that was the beginning of my effort to work through the pain." Jen also demonstrated through her patience that David could talk for himself. "She wouldn't help me," David says. "I would be stuttering trying to order lunch and I'd kick her under the table to help me order. She would say out loud, 'No, you have what it takes to communicate effectively – you speak just fine.'"

David's father thought that Jennifer was the perfect mate for his son. He was so happy when they became engaged. A few months later, Antonio Salazar passed away. David was the last person his father talked to before he died, asking his son never to forget him. "When he died, I laid right on top of his body like a baby," David shares. "I laid right on top of him. I had finally understood what he had taught me. He had taught me to be a man." That night David Salazar knew what being a man was all about. "It wasn't about how much liquor you could drink, how much weight you could lift, or how many tough stories you could tell. Being a man was about helping others and not worrying about yourself."

David approached the priest and told him he wanted to deliver the eulogy at his father's funeral. The priest and David's mother were both concerned that he really wouldn't be able to express his feelings under such emotional stress. The response was consistent with the new David, without pretense, guile, or mask. "I want to give Dad the biggest gift I could possibly give him now. The thing I fear most: speaking." During the funeral, David delivered a wonderful 10-minute eulogy titled "I Remember." And he didn't stutter on one word. From that day on, David promised himself he would never fear speaking again. He knows that his heart will pound and he will get nervous when speaking, but he is secure in the knowledge of who he is and that he controls this disorder, it doesn't control him. "My communication style doesn't describe who I am," David boldly proclaims. "What describes who I am is how I lead my life, how I love my family and my children, and how I love my God. That is what describes me."

The mask that was fashioned and re-fashioned so many times has totally dissolved. David is not the angry, tough guy with all the connections in high school; he is not the poor student, afraid to participate; he is not the man who will say anything to avoid a stutter; he is not the man who avoids a challenge because of fear; he is not Juan, Ted, Mike, Fred, Allen, Joe, or even Chico; he is David Salazar, the man who believes he has a destiny in life to help others by sharing his own life experience. His stuttering is no longer a debilitating challenge, but a gift to help others.

David is now the BOOST Coordinator at the Sandy, Utah Operations Center for Discover Financial Services. His willingness to share his inspirational life story with others who are experiencing challenges and heartache in their lives is a powerful validation of what David's father continually taught him: "Never forget where you came from; if you forget where you came from you cannot learn; if you cannot learn you cannot teach; so please never forget where you came from so others may learn."

The cold, dark, clammy mask that David Salazar tried so

hard to live within has given way to a bright, sunlit world of opportunity. Not only for David, Jen, and the boys, but also for hundreds of grateful BOOST graduates who have felt the warmth of his caring soul.

Ginger

◆ ·╫═◆ఋ◎◖◗═╫· ◆

N ew York, New York! The Big Apple! If you can make it here, you can make it anywhere. The most vibrant city in the world was pulsating with activity. Although just in her early twenties, Ginger Lott was infused with the vitality of this amazing place. The energy was so robust she could almost wrap her arms around it. And yet, she knew that something was wrong.

Ginger had traveled to New York to visit her sister, who was attending Columbia University. After observing the difficulty Ginger was having with her right leg, her sister, a physical therapist, put everything in motion by advising Ginger to get an appointment with a neurologist immediately upon her return to Phoenix. She was concerned that the problems with walking and slurred speech that Ginger had displayed might be indicative of some type of neurological disorder.

Since Ginger belonged to a controlled health insurance plan, she first visited her primary care physician to obtain a referral to a neurologist as her sister had recommended. The doctor did not agree with the "amateur" diagnosis and began a protocol to uncover the true source of the problem. After evaluating x-rays and other tests, it was decided that Ginger had a slipped disc in her back. Potent medication was prescribed to control the advancing pain. The medication, however, just made Ginger more dizzy and nauseated.

More than a month of no progress motivated the doctor to issue a referral to an orthopedic surgeon, even though Ginger was increasingly vocal about her desire to see a neurologist. The orthopedic physician found no problems within his area of specialty so the patient was referred back for further consultation. After almost six months, Ginger was finally given the go-ahead to meet with a neurological specialist per the original suggestion.

The symptoms indicated either multiple sclerosis or a congenital problem with the size of the hole where the brain stem fits. A brain tumor was considered an outside chance but not very likely. An initial MRI, however, revealed that Ginger did indeed have a tumor approximately the size of a small peach located in an inoperable area of her brain. Further pathology tests confirmed that the tumor was malignant. She was told that it had most likely been growing for 10 or 15 years.

Ginger's first reaction was probably quite typical of patients who find they have inoperable malignancies: shock and disbelief. "I couldn't understand what the whole purpose was," Ginger says. "I knew that there had to be a reason, I just didn't know what it was. To be honest with you, I still don't know what it is."

She felt angry and sorry for herself. Her natural, happy demeanor transformed almost instantly into sadness and fear. "Right away you think you are going to die," Ginger remembers. "Well, you know what? We are all going to die. It just depends on how and when."

Ginger had enjoyed a relatively normal life up to the time of her diagnosis. After her parents were divorced, she moved from Los Angeles to Phoenix to live with her dad. She was in her mid-teens at the time. She later graduated with an associate's degree from college and went to work for an insurance company, where she worked until her illness made it impossible for her to continue.

When she was growing up, Ginger was always sort of clumsy. No one ever gave a second thought to the idea that it might be the result of some kind of medical problem, certainly not a brain tumor.

Nevertheless, that's what it was and the rules of the game had changed completely. At a time of life when most young adults are just beginning to realize the achievement of some of their most important dreams and objectives, Ginger was faced with an almost total loss of hope for the future. She battled depression and a sense of hopelessness. "I can't really describe what that's like," Ginger shares. "It just gave me a feeling of giving up. I thought, 'This is it! There is no use in even trying.'"

When friends and family were first told of her condition, they were shocked and very concerned. Most reacted with stone silence, not knowing what to say or how to respond. Their temporary paralysis was fleeting and quickly replaced itself with an active support system that sustained Ginger during those early days.

At first, she wanted people to feel sorry for her. This was a big deal. This was her life that hung in the balance. A little pity in this situation surely couldn't hurt anyone. As she grew to understand the nature of her illness and watched as people struggled to treat her in a "normal" way, Ginger realized that what she really wanted was to be treated like everyone else. She was still the same person. She still had the same needs and dreams for the future. The pain and discomfort created by her illness, coupled with the dependency that she began to feel, helped Ginger to understand how important it was for her to nurture her independent spirit.

A mega-dose of chemotherapy was introduced through an IV injection as the first step in her treatment. The process took about an hour and caused her to be very nauseous. The chemo was followed by a heavy dose of radiation that was done twice every day for six weeks. Ginger needed steroids during this regimen to help keep the swelling down. Her body blew up like a balloon and she couldn't get enough to eat. Her appetite zoomed into the stratosphere as she ate whatever was readily available.

The radiation was accomplished through the use of a mask

that was formed to Ginger's face. The mask was then strapped down so she couldn't move her head. Targets were placed on the side of the mask to precisely focus the radiation on the tumor area. As her weight gain, precipitated by the steroids, began to add girth to her face, the mask became tight and uncomfortable. Breathing was laborious during the latter portion of this process.

About halfway through the treatment, Ginger suddenly was unable to walk by herself. She needed someone to lean on and steady her movement. Support became more to Ginger than just a phone call, a card, or a visit. She needed physical support to even move.

The doctors remained optimistic during the active treatment. They never believed that the radiation would actually shrink the tumor, but they were confident that any growth could be retarded. Their optimism was valid. In five years since diagnosis, the tumor has not grown at all; nor has it shrunk. It cannot be surgically removed because it is entwined with the brain stem that controls all functions of the body. In reality, Ginger lives each day with her malignant brain tumor as a permanent companion.

Since completing her treatment protocol, Ginger has had to overcome several side effects of both the tumor and the treatment. She suffered for a long time with violent headaches that would last for days without relief. Strong painkillers eventually conquered the worst of these painful episodes.

Her short-term memory has also been permanently altered. "I learned to be more patient with people than I used to be," she says. "I have to take my time to do things. I have to do things while I'm thinking about them, because if I wait until later, I will totally forget."

Perhaps the most devastating blow to Ginger's sense of autonomy is her inability to drive a car. She feels that most people take this everyday occurrence for granted. "When it is taken away from you," Ginger says, "it's like a part of your independence has been removed. I just can't say, 'Oh, I need to go to the store' and jump in the car and go. That is still one of the hardest things for me to deal with."

Walking also continues to be a challenge. Although she can now walk without the need of physical support, hiking or walking for exercise is not possible. Ginger walks to get someplace, never for recreation. She also must avoid lifting and other physical activities that could aggravate her delicate balance.

The news of her diagnosis, coupled with the strenuous treatment and debilitating side effects, caused Ginger to lose confidence in herself. She spent a lot of time watching TV and pretty much became a couch potato. Nothing motivated her, probably because she perceived herself to be worthless. She felt like there was nothing she could do, so why even try?

Ginger's father recognized the deterioration in his daughter's emotional and physical condition. He realized that she needed to become active again, so he encouraged her to get out of bed and start the process of finding a job she could do. When the reservoir of personal worth is drained dry, common, everyday activities, like job-hunting, become almost intolerable. Ginger felt betrayed by her father's encouragement. She didn't feel she had the strength or the ability to work. In her mind, her toolbox of skills had been depleted because of all the physical and mental limitations, some of which were real and others perceived.

As she began the process of looking for a job, Ginger experienced a great deal of rejection. She became even more discouraged as she exhausted all of her alternatives. No one seemed willing to take a chance on her. She was sure that the roadblock to productive employment was her brain tumor, and there was nothing she could do about that. While it was true that she had certain limitations, the skills she had learned in three years of full-time employment in a progressive office environment were still intact. She still thought she was capable of making a contribution, but employers were not willing to give her the opportunity to show what she could do.

Her father continued to prod her, trying to help her get over the rejection and disappointment she continued to encounter. The tactic caused friction between the two. He knew what was best for Ginger, but she thought, "I have this brain tumor and you are pushing me too hard. Who do you think you are? I have all these problems and you don't acknowledge them."

In retrospect, Ginger realizes the value of her father's perseverance. He understood what she needed. Now they both understand how important it was for him to keep up the pressure. However, Ginger intensely resented it at the time. They had serious discussions about their relationship and how his behavior was eroding her sense of worth even more.

Ginger did not give up. Even though her job search was causing a rift with her father and severe frustration for her, the value of finding a job was kindled deep inside. The quest for someone to validate her sense of worth motivated her continued search. Somehow, she developed some powerful inner strength through the process that provided a rudder for her life and helped stabilize her emotional ship.

Finally, Ginger found a volunteer job with the Humane Society. She had always liked animals but since she could do little lifting or other physical chores, her role was confined to basic paper shuffling. It just wasn't challenging enough for her. She had so much more to give.

Four long years had passed while Ginger was outside of the workplace. She looked everywhere for a job, turned over every rock, made every contact and every phone call she could think of. Most prospective employers wouldn't even return her calls. Her disability had branded her forever, or so it seemed. The emotional tension began to exceed the physical strain. "I didn't want people to feel sorry for me," she recalls. "I just wanted them to understand me and give me a chance. An inoperable brain tumor that affects my balance, coordination, and speech should not confine me to a life on the couch watching TV."

While Ginger was still volunteering at the Humane Society, her counselor at DES (Department of Economic Security) told her about a new program called BOOST. By this time, Ginger was anxious to reach out for anything that would open the evasive door of opportunity. Here was another possibility, but there had been so many possibilities that had evaporated.

She went through the interview process and was accepted into the program. Immediately, a tidal wave of optimism swelled up inside of her. "These people at Discover Card really care," Ginger says. "They get it. They are interested in my abilities, not my disabilities."

Attitude and self-confidence are delicate components of the human spirit. When a person develops a sense of worth that is encouraged and fortified by the confidence and trust of others, an amazing transformation occurs. What was perceived as daunting suddenly mutates to feasible; what was unreachable becomes obtainable. Having the invigorating feeling of accomplishment causes self-confidence to soar; latent potential surges into reality.

Such was the case with Ginger Lott. Positive reinforcement energized her dormant skills. Given a chance to perform, she became a star. Ginger was hired full time by Discover Card on her BOOST graduation day. Her mood was a combination of relieved and ecstatic. "Whoever said that Disneyland is the 'friendliest place on earth' obviously has never been to Discover Card," Ginger believes.

The future is uncertain for this courageous young woman. Ginger has no idea what the prognosis is. She doesn't ask and doesn't want to know. "I could walk out in the middle of the street and get hit by a truck," she says. "No one is really sure of what tomorrow might bring."

Ginger used to think there was no future for her. She didn't feel she would ever be the same person again. Most would agree that Ginger isn't the same person. She's even better, more compassionate and more productive than ever before. She has endured great physical pain and emotional anguish on this road to self-fulfillment.

While remnants of the past still dot her path, Ginger's life inspires all who are touched by it. "It is never hopeless," she counsels. "You can rise above anything. You just need to have faith that things will work out for you. Of course, you need to put in some work yourself, but it can be done."

Why do these things happen? What is the purpose of life's challenges? Why has this vibrant young woman in the prime of her life been given such a test? Answers are often hard to find. Perhaps our challenge is to learn all the questions and the answers will ultimately take care of themselves.

The cliché, "We can learn from the experience of others," has never been more true than the heartfelt message of the following poem titled "Please," written by Ginger Lott.

PLEASE

Please don't be afraid
to ask me about "it."
Silence is worse.
Please don't be afraid
to ask me how I feel
today.
Please understand that
I won't always see the
"bright side" of things,
there isn't always one.
Please don't be afraid
to give me a hug –
I won't break, I promise.
Please continue to show
your caring,
understanding,
and support –
I could use some right
now.
Please just be my friend.

Susan M.

"This can't be happening to me after 36 years of waiting . . . " Susan caught herself in mid-sentence. "Sure," she thought, "other people have serious problems but this is the worst of nature's cruel deceptions."

The doctor had just told Susan and husband, Randy, that her troubled pregnancy was not what it seemed to be. Rather than a developing fetus growing into their first child, Susan was devastated to learn that she had gestational trophoblastic disease, more commonly known as a molar pregnancy. The symptoms of pregnancy that she had experienced for the previous several months had been a hoax. Something went wrong at time of conception; rogue cells had mutated into a mole that formed in her uterus.

To this point, the mimicked symptoms had generated great euphoria. All were convinced that this was, indeed, the long-sought-after pregnancy that both Susan and Randy had so desperately wanted. But the HCG count in her blood, the hormone measurement used to detect pregnancy, was fraudulent. It had been triggered by the mutant cells, not by a maturing fetus.

An initial medical concern was that Susan was losing the baby through a miscarriage. Multiple blood tests, however, soon confirmed a molar pregnancy, which was also diagnosed as malignant. The word "cancer" was so remotely connected to the excitement of the previous few months that a first brush with its potential consequences was superceded by the grief of the non-pregnancy. Reality arrived with potency in the following days, riding a wave of discouragement and newly-hatched fear.

Discouragement and fear of the future were not new emotions for Susan. Her father, with whom she shared a very close relationship, developed a terminal disease when Susan was 11 years old. He passed away a year later. The experience was devastating for this tomboy who loved sports and played army with her neighborhood buddies. She felt a strong connection to her father. His death created a void that took years to fill. She often thinks about him and what her life would be like today had he lived.

With their father gone, the expectation was clearly established by Susan's widowed, 36-year-old working mother that all the children would share the everyday family duties. Being the oldest of three siblings, Susan was saddled with additional responsibility, which, at times, caused her to feel emotionally overwhelmed.

The family's financial life was difficult. There was no stalwart stream of income to balance the expanding needs of three children growing into adolescence. For Susan, the financial deficiency was particularly pointed. Other girls her age were captivated by designer clothes, jewelry, and assorted trinkets, luxuries that were mostly out of reach for Susan and her siblings. She understood, however, her mother's struggle to provide the basic necessities of life. "Mom actually did very well considering what we were working with," Susan recounts. "She tried hard to give us the things that were necessary and then some."

Susan was her own person. She liked being different. "I never wanted to be a cookie cutter of somebody else," she says. "I distinctly know what is me and that can be good for some people and kind of strange to others." In short, Susan marched to the beat of her own drummer. She liked having an opinion and did her best to help others see her point of view. Some people said she enjoyed arguing; Susan prefers to view it as an animated exchange of ideas.

The high school years were a very dark time. Susan developed a resilient exterior that could be perceived as caustic or angry, certainly emotional, as she battled her personal demons while trying to understand the depression that was engulfing her. "It was typical for me to take some Valium 20 or 25 years ago to overcome the feelings that I was having," Susan remembers. "I struggled with it starting at age 15. It made me a total basket case."

Her eclectic personality attracted many different types of

friends, but a few close relationships taught Susan the value of friend-ships that both nourish and nurture. She was especially sustained through some difficult times by the love of a special girlfriend who remains a powerful source of strength to this day. The two pals pro-vided a reciprocal support system for each other as they forged their way through the emotional peaks and valleys of adolescent life.

Other challenges of a more personal nature raided Susan's world as she grew to womanhood. She holds the memory of those experiences in her most intimate space, along with a few vivid images of specific situations where her sensibilities were offended. One recollection that forced her to ask, "Why me?" was the occa-sion of her graduation from high school.

Traditionally, everyone got a new dress for graduation. Susan's busy mother was making hers. Several of the girls decided they would express their rebellious spirit by wearing jeans under their robes instead of a dress. They got together to make a pact. Since Susan's dress was not yet finished because of the huge demands on her mother's time, this seemed like a great way for Susan to avoid the embarrassment of not having a new outfit.

As is normally the case in such situations, only Susan and her friend ended up wearing jeans. They were pulled out of line by the school counselor and not allowed to walk in the processional. Because the female graduation robes were white, the dresses had to be white as well. After the students had been seated in the audi-ence, a snooty girl near where Susan was sitting loudly quipped, "Oh, it's a shame you can't even afford a white slip."

Susan's friend tried to console her by saying, "Forget it. It's none of their business." Susan, however, was badly hurt. This was an important moment in her life. The images of the previous several years swelled up in her memory. She began to cry as the emotion overcame her independent nature. "Why me?" she asked herself, "This just isn't fair." The rebel was reduced to emotional rubble.

Susan Blair-Mather is a contradiction. She is kind, compassionate, sensitive, and caring. There are times when her tender feelings and caring nature are offended by the unkind comments or behavior of others. And yet she also has a tendency to be a little dark, a little cynical. She rides the full spectrum of life's emotional roller coaster, bouncing off the walls and bursting with laughter one minute to a more melancholy place where tears easily flow the next.

At 17, graduated from high school, Susan began her work career as part-time Christmas help at Sears. Six months later she became a full-time employee. In 1985, she transferred, along with just 20 other people, into the new accounts department for the credit card Sears had introduced, called Discover Card.

Two of the vocational values that prevailed at the time Susan entered the work force were stability and loyalty. A person either went to college or found a good company that would be the foundation for a lifetime career. The move to Discover Card, even though it was a new division of the same company, was a 180-degree turn. The background she had received at Sears was a real advantage as she embarked on a new career journey in customer service, new accounts, and training. Although the change was somewhat frightening, she knew that this fresh opportunity had the potential to build on her acquired skills while serving as a catalyst to carry her as far as she wanted to go.

Change has always been difficult for Susan. She is particularly methodical in her decision-making process, weighing the alternatives and evaluating the benefits until the exercise sometimes becomes very laborious. The change in employment, however, was given birth concurrently with the ending of a bad relationship. The direction of Susan's life was dramatically altered in one giant swoop. Life became both a little exciting and a little intimidating at the same time.

The job was very enjoyable for Susan. "I have always felt comfortable around other people," she says. "Not so much in a social situation like a party or the bar scene, but I have always felt comfortable in the work environment, regardless of the level of the employees I was around." Since she has an unusual ability to adapt her communication style to help other people feel comfortable, most of her associates, from janitors to top managers, have found it easy to talk with Susan.

She has a lot of chemistry about her. Her charismatic personality entices and attracts while creating a safe harbor for friends and associates to enjoy. Susan is candid and direct, with a positive flair for the diplomatic, often considered the queen of diplomacy at work. While not necessarily considered a politically correct woman, she has a gift to articulate what needs to be said in a painless and inoffensive way.

Her compassionate and loving demeanor is not a put-on; she is an honest reflection of her genuine persona. People around her quickly recognize the honesty of the image they encounter. They are also confronted with a well-developed talent for sarcasm, an outgrowth of a cynical wit born of the protection mechanism Susan developed as a young girl.

As early as a sixth-grade slumber party, Susan realized the value of offsetting hurtful barbs with a caustic quip. Hurt could be diluted with humor, she decided, especially if the humor carried a sharp edge. Her sense of humor became her shield: her sensitive nature protected by a veneer of timely sarcasm that functionally deflected any hurt generated by the comments or behavior of another. She soon found that she was funny. Not only did her sarcastic wit serve to protect her, it made people laugh – with her, not at her.

Many associates perceive Susan to be anal because of her inherent ability to organize details and follow through to successful completion with the most demanding projects. Susan doesn't necessarily picture herself as anal, perhaps due to the diverse nature of her self-image. She does, however, recognize her commitment to organization, order, and achievement. Getting something accomplished with efficiency and style is the trademark of her professional performance.

She also recognizes the baggage she carries. "It is real," she emphasizes. "It is simple reality that there are demons and baggage that everyone carries, but you find through that a way to express yourself." The stark contrasts between tenderness and sarcasm, enthusiasm and cynicism, organization and spontaneity, all provide a backdrop for the ultimate contradiction that exists in Susan's life between a caring heart and her darker side.

When the fiasco of a failed pregnancy began the transformation to the reality of a serious, even life-threatening disease, Susan's cynicism was fueled once more. Up to that time, she had never been sick. She had never been to the emergency ward, had never broken a bone, never had a stitch, and never had a major illness other than the typical childhood diseases. Now, faced with the prospect of a long, rigorous treatment protocol, Susan was psychologically unprepared.

Frazzled emotions and disappointment were offset by the unwavering support of her husband. His sustaining influence and positive reinforcement were instrumental in helping Susan prepare for the impending battle. The initial procedure was a simple D&C to clean out the unwanted cells, followed by a mild form of chemotherapy. Her blood was carefully monitored during this six-month period. The results were initially successful as her blood count continued to go down, actually hovering in the normal range for a short time.

Without warning, blood test data shot out of range requiring an immediate response. The chemotherapy dosage was increased significantly, causing normal, but debilitating, side effects such as extreme nausea and loss of hair. Susan also had several different D&C procedures as well as a more invasive surgery to remove the cancerous cells in an attempt to arrest their development. Several uncomfortable MRIs were conducted due to serious concern that the cancer cells would metastasize (migrate) from the uterus to the brain or lungs.

After about nine months, Susan was introduced into a full-blown, hard-core chemo program that required weekly treatments. She was in and out of the hospital for months. Some of the treatments were done on an outpatient basis and some required hospitalization due to the strength of the drugs or the reactions that followed.

The treatment was brutal. Still, through it all, Susan was firmly focused on the goal of saving her uterus because she wanted to have children so badly. The first specialist recommended a hysterectomy right away. Since Susan was adamantly opposed to that solution, the chemotherapy and D&C alternatives were presented as possibilities to avoid removing her uterus.

A referral to a blood cancer specialist resulted in an increase in the dosage of Susan's chemo treatments. A gynecologist from the Arthur G. James Cancer Hospital and Research Institute in Columbus, Ohio subsequently provided a final diagnosis. He presented two clear alternatives: First, have a hysterectomy and save your life; or, second, die. "I had never thought of it as killing me until then," Susan recalls.

Susan and Randy began a frantic search on the Internet to gather more information. One doctor had earlier told them that the medical community had developed little knowledge about gestational trophoblastic disease since the 1950s. Their Internet investigation confirmed the doctor's diagnosis: Without a hysterectomy, Susan risked losing her life.

She had been through the entire chemotherapy protocol three different times. Twice it appeared the treatments had been successful. When Susan fell ill a third time, the options were very clear. "I think that in your mind you have a lot of plans and you start thinking about what the future will be and having a family," she says. "I told Randy I never realized until we couldn't have children that you look at other people's children and see pieces of the parents, and you want to put together the good pieces of both of us."

It was a very emotional time. Susan remembers, "At the time I would joke and say, 'Okay, I can live and have a hysterectomy.' You try to keep a sense of humor about it. I really didn't want to die." The decision had no option; the alternatives had all been explored. Susan courageously entered the James Institute to have her uterus removed and to save her life.

Randy remained very supportive during the hospital stay and recuperation. Although her husband couldn't understand the depth of Susan's disappointment, he constantly reassured her that, even though they couldn't have biological children, they would look into adoption when she was emotionally prepared.

The pursuit of a child to adopt became a positive antidote to a developing depression that Susan was experiencing. "I used to think that being a mother was kind of a special club," she says, "That unless you had a child, you really couldn't be part of it. I was a member of the cancer club. Even though there is a good feeling that comes from knowing that you have fought this and won, it does change you."

Susan and Randy had made great plans to accommodate their own child in their lives. They had put themselves in an appropriate financial position, organized their careers, and had begun the journey to the realization of their dreams. They were golden candidates to become adoptive parents. The possibility heightened Susan's positive expectancy.

An unborn child carried by an unmarried teenager was found. The process was set in motion and all the details were settled. The young biological mother was committed to providing a quality life for her child. The baby would become part of Susan and Randy's family at birth. A new euphoria was beginning to germinate for Susan. Perhaps this is the way it was supposed to be all the time. Susan felt that she could love and care for this child as if it were her own. She was finally going to get a chance to join the mother's club.

A few days after the baby was born, the birth mother changed her mind and decided to raise the child herself. While the girl had every right to make that choice, the devastation that her decision created was incredible for Susan. The dark cloud she had valiantly fought through for most of her life settled even lower. The depression returned, but this time with even more intensity.

Another abrupt change of emotions was too much. She had made the return trip from elation to defeat on so many occasions that her system went into overload. At times, Susan confronted a huge challenge to just get out of bed. Medication was prescribed that helps control the emotional gyrations. "I look at it kind of like diabetics need their insulin," she says, "a chemical imbalance. I am now at a point where I can recognize when I am heading downhill. I know what to do and I do it."

Susan received the good news on her birthday that her blood count continued to be normal. This announcement was particularly important because it was her clean bill of health, having been more than two years since the surgery. Doctors feel assured that she has been successfully cured of the cancer. "I told several people at work and called friends and family to share the news," Susan remembers. "I felt like I was saying the words but not feeling what was actually happening. I don't know if it ever sank in to the point that I felt truly elated or overwhelmed. I had heard that everything is going well so many times."

Susan goes back each year for a complete check-up. She believes that once you have experienced something like this, "It always hangs over your head. The question that you continually ask yourself is, 'What if something happens again?'"

Getting in touch with one's own mortality and experiencing the G-forces generated by life's dynamics has a profound impact on personal goals and objectives. Susan did a lot of soul searching during and after her trials to determine what it was she really wanted out of this earthly existence. She continued to question what difference her well-performed job was making. How was she really contributing to the welfare of society, the world, or even her own community? It wasn't that she felt she could save the world; it was the realization that she had more to give and needed the personal satisfaction of giving it.

Susan loved being a part of the training department at Discover Card but her position was outside of the classroom. In order to relieve some of the stress, she decided to go part-time while she determined what it was that she wanted.

Shortly after, while sitting in a senior staff meeting, the decision to begin the BOOST program in Columbus was announced. Susan feels that she received her "calling" right there in the meeting. "I felt like I was on a mission. My manager and I left the meeting, walked to his office, and I said, 'I want to know more about this. I want to be a part of it. I want to do this.'"

Susan was given a portion of the BOOST training manual along with some other information. She took it home that evening and read every word of the history, the manual, everything that was given to her. "I just felt like all of a sudden I got my calling," Susan says. "It was a religious experience." There wasn't a question in her mind that started with "if." All of the questions had to do with when, how, where, and what.

Assuming the BOOST coordinator role required Susan to step down from a training manager position to become a training specialist. She feels the move was a wonderful decision for her. "It is helping people, but it is more helping them to see what is out there," she believes. "I like knowing that I can do something to help people feel better about themselves."

Susan Mather has gone through a great deal of physical and emotional trauma in her life. She can truly empathize with people who have challenges of their own. "I was raised on a dollar something an hour by a hard-working mother with help from Social Security. We didn't have a lot, but I wouldn't change anything. That has made me who I am and has made me appreciate how people make silly assumptions about people with challenges. I never judge a book by its cover anymore."

Parents, teachers, clergy, work supervisors, and especially professional motivators often talk about using the experiences we are given in life as a foundation to launch personal achievement. Few of us really follow that valuable advice. Instead, we most often sulk, feel sorry for ourselves, and retreat into the protective shell of excuse and rationalization. Susan has combined her wonderful, natural skills with the lessons she has learned from her own life to become a builder, to reach out to those who need a helping hand.

An old adage suggests that when you give of yourself, you get more back than you give. Susan understands the power of that statement. Each day the wisdom of the words on her bulletin board penetrates her heart: "We are here to make life easier for those around us." Her commitment is to help those her life touches internalize the most important lesson she has learned from what she has gone through: "Define who you are and what you want and never be detoured or put off track by what other people think."

Susan believes, "It is especially important for women to believe in themselves and work towards accomplishing whatever they want, rather than thinking that somebody is going to come along and do it for them." She realizes the power of positive example and holds sacred the responsibility she has been given to be a catalyst for change for many who have lost hope or see no opportunity.

Nature's ultimate deception for Susan was the heartbreak of having cancer instead of a baby. "Sometimes I get frustrated," she honestly shares. "We thought we did it all the right way. You get married, get to know each other, buy a house, and start planning for children. All of a sudden you are saying, 'Why can a 16-year-old have a baby?' But I know that life isn't always fair."

Today, after the dew has settled on a vast field of opportunity, Susan has transformed that frustration into compassionate understanding. "I have let my anger go," Susan now declares, "and hope that if there is a young woman in class who is a single parent, that I can help her see her own potential so that she doesn't end up a welfare mom. I want to help her be the best parent that she can be and successful in whatever she wants to accomplish."

The cycle has been completed for Susan. Tragedy, pain, and depression have been exchanged for hope, happiness, and unconditional love.

Paul

T his is a story of transformation, a process that, to some degree, everyone experiences during the evolutionary journey through life. Personal metamorphosis occurs in different ways for different reasons. It is frequently the result of natural growth and development. A baby learns to walk by first holding its head up and then struggling to roll over. After standing with the support of a chair and finally balancing with confidence, a first exhilarating step is taken to the cheers of adoring family and friends. A child's world, and often that of its parents, is never quite the same from that moment forward.

At the same time that muscles are strengthening, bones are hardening and other physical attributes are maturing, verbal language also begins to blossom. A child mimics the sounds most often heard in its environment by using its mouth, tongue, and voice to form rudiments of words. Mouth dexterity, voice box, and brain ultimately become synchronized to produce simple, recognizable words that are celebrated with great fanfare. The process of learning to communicate has begun.

While many customary growth factors occur almost involuntarily, barriers to development sometimes interrupt the natural flow. Children confronted with challenges in their quest to run and talk like the other kids often feel ostracized. Adults not born with a marvelous singing voice, a keen intellect, or great athletic ability tend to consider their options to be limited. When children and adults come to realize that they have a significant amount of control over their destiny, a broad spectrum of previously unrecognized opportunity unfolds before them. Understanding precedes hope; hope gives birth to self-esteem; self-esteem nurtures confidence; and confidence is the breeding ground for personal growth and transformation.

Paul Murphy knows the process all too well. He has invested a huge amount of emotional capital in understanding the barriers to his own development, and the subsequent conquering of his particular challenges. His transformation is an inspirational story of congenital limitations, bankrupt self-esteem, personal courage, and ultimate victory over oneself.

Born with cerebral palsy affecting the left side of his body, Paul is unable to grasp or feel with his left hand. "If I had a pencil in my hand and I didn't know I was carrying it, I would probably drop it," he confides. His left foot curls in, causing him to walk with a slight gait, a challenge that created some emotional discomfort as he was growing up. He is also paralyzed on the right side of his face. Although the vision in his right eye has always been extremely limited, a cataract will not be removed due to the paralysis. Deafness in his right ear has required another significant adjustment, but perhaps the biggest attack on Paul's self-esteem has come from the visible effect the paralysis has had on his right facial muscles. He has very little control over those important muscles, especially when he smiles.

The total picture, then, includes a person with limited strength in his left arm and leg, blind in his right eye, deaf in his right ear, and a partial facial paralysis. What the picture does not immediately reflect is the intensity of this young man, nor the struggle he has waged to overcome the challenges that have been part of his world since birth.

From his earliest recollections, Paul always wanted to play baseball. He was never able to fulfill that dream, because of his convoluted disabilities, but experiencing a huge disappointment with baseball opened another door to soccer. His father became a coach with an instructional youth soccer league to help his son participate in a sport that would provide some physical activity. Paul became very involved. He enjoyed playing the game but also made some new friends. He continues to be a "huge fanatic" about the sport of his youth.

"It's the way things work," Paul philosophizes. "If I could have played baseball, I probably would not have even known about soccer. Small instances in your life can direct you on a whole different path that you never thought you'd go on." That path for Paul represents the germination of the skill to adapt, a nurtured talent that has served him well as his life has unfolded.

The realization that he was a little different from the other kids was an evolutionary process. As a small child in school, Paul couldn't understand why he was in the special education class with kids who were in wheelchairs, on crutches, or had other visible disabilities. Later, while playing sandlot baseball with neighborhood friends, he recognized that he was not able to catch the ball like the other kids and he always struck out when he tried to hit the ball. Gradually the stark reality came into focus: Paul was not like the other guys. "But then mom and dad sat me down and said, 'this is how it is,'" he remembers.

Those early years were bittersweet for Paul. He had some good friends who included him in activities and became a valuable support system. He also had a family that was a constant source of strength. "My dad was the best," Paul says, "I had a couple of friends whose dads weren't there for them all the time, not like my dad. I don't know where I'd be without my mom and my dad and my sister. Every chance I get I thank them."

Still, regular rejection in childhood grew to be traumatic. The roots of negative self-esteem corrupted his development process. Paul began very early to feel inferior. He crawled into a protective shell that shut out some of the confusion he felt. By high school, he had become very shy and quiet. Functions and activities escaped his normal routine. "I think that was my way of saying, 'I don't want to hear it,'" Paul suggests. "If I don't hear people talk about me and make fun of me, it's like it doesn't happen."

Questions about the future started to grow in Paul's mind. What am I going to do? What is going to happen to me? How will I support myself? These were all important questions he began to consider. Paul was confused. He had been very organized with a positive attitude until about the seventh grade. His room was always orderly with clothes and shoes systematically arranged. Now, he had evolved into a "Messy Marvin" after being a neat freak in his younger years. His attitude had also deteriorated into a rigid "can't do" or "won't do" mentality.

Paul saw himself as lacking ambition and discipline. He didn't really want to continue his education but he didn't have a job or any prospects that remotely interested him. During his junior year in high school, he began seeing the first of a long line of psychiatrists in a futile attempt to rebuild his negative self-perception. "I sorta lied to that counselor a little bit," Paul says. "What he said really didn't interest me. I was sorta ho-hum about it. Later I realized that these people can't help me when I don't want to help myself."

Paul had always wanted to go into the military. He saw that avenue as a solution to correct his attitude and discipline issues. Unfortunately, he did not qualify due to his extensive physical limitations. This new, although expected, rejection prompted additional passivity. Paul became a full-time "couch potato" after high school. With nothing to do and little ambition, he spent his life basically wasting away. He did enter college, where his performance was acceptable during the first semester. Subsequently, as with every other endeavor in his life, Paul's educational achievement went rapidly downhill. He quit school and returned to his inactive lifestyle.

Personal performance is almost always directly proportional to how a person visualizes himself. Paul's self-image was entirely based in defeat and rejection, notwithstanding the support and commitment of a caring family. He saw himself as an abject failure as well as unworthy of success. He considered any attempt to modify his behavior to be futile. He completely lost confidence in the most important element that could reverse his karma: himself.

Disappointment defeated hope in a classic confrontation after Paul dropped out of college. He managed to focus his energy long enough to find an entry-level job at a department store. However, not long after being hired, Paul was involved in a serious automobile accident that left him with only two transportation options: walking or riding his bike to work.

The discouragement intensified as Paul searched the job market for something better to do. Because he knew the value of a first impression, Paul didn't feel comfortable with selling himself on a written application or in an interview. He would exaggerate the number of applications he was actually submitting, when asked by his mother or father how the job hunt was going. His parents became more concerned about Paul's lack of success in life and the

lack of enthusiasm they observed. "I would say I was lacking mentally what other people my age had," Paul believes. "I didn't know
how to act around people or how to stay focused. I knew I had to
get a job. I had to move somewhere. I had to make a life for
myself but I was realizing no success."

Gradually, Paul started to fit the pieces together. He
embarked on the long pilgrimage to understand who he was and
how he could be successful. His picture of himself slowly began to
clear. He was able to realize success at simple tasks like the jobs he
found working part time in light manufacturing and the hotel
industry. His transformation was starting to take form.

Paul began helping his father coach the soccer team he had
previously played on. He felt like he belonged. He was able to talk
strategy with his dad and give advice to the players. During one
practice, the ball was kicked well beyond the fence surrounding the
field, rolling rapidly down a slight hill. In hot pursuit of the errant
ball, Paul decided to jump the fence rather than try to reach the
gate that was 15-20 yards away. He landed well on his left leg but
his right leg buckled under the pressure. Paul blacked out, learning
a few minutes later that he had broken both the tibia and fibula of
his right leg.

Because of his cerebral palsy, the left side of Paul's body had
always caused disruption to a normal lifestyle. Now, in an instant,
he had severely damaged his right leg. A rod was installed along
with a large number of screws to stabilize the bones. The work Paul
had so diligently struggled to find had to be abandoned for a while.

Bills he had accumulated in his quest for independence began to pile up. His parents helped him but it just wasn't the same as doing for himself.

After the injury, Paul's father introduced him to a friend, who invited Paul to help deliver newspapers in the morning. The feeling of exhilaration that came from this simple responsibility started a chain reaction. Paul understood that he could make at least a limited contribution. His understanding became the precursor to a rekindling of his hope for the future. He felt more positive about himself. He was refreshed and motivated to find a better job.

Perceived discrimination was an ever-present element of every job search. Potential employers were sometimes skeptical of his ability to get the job done. All he was looking for was a chance to prove himself. "When I got into a job I really wasn't discriminated against, that I really saw," Paul remembers. "Maybe I didn't look at it the same way. Maybe I didn't care because I knew what my job was and I did it. That's one of my strong points. I've always been a good worker. I'll give 110% even though I can't use my left hand or see out of my right eye."

Finally, a better opportunity came when Paul found employment at the Christiana Hilton Hotel, a job he held for more than five years. Because of his hard work and commitment to his job, Paul was recognized as employee of the month. Shortly after receiving the award, he was faced with a serious situation at the hotel that required quick action to avert a tragedy.

Paul's mother had dropped him off at work that wintry

morning. Most of the city had ground to a screeching halt due to the fierce storm that had invaded the area. Although he was 45 minutes late arriving, Paul was virtually the only person in his department, the hotel laundry, who was able to get to work. After taking the customary morning break, Paul returned to the laundry area to find a small fire burning next to the ceiling. He reacted quickly by getting to a phone to call the hotel operator, advising her to contact the fire department. He then ran back into the laundry with a fire extinguisher and was able to get the blaze under control. A major accident was neutralized because Paul had made the effort to get to work that day.

He was pleased with his contribution. The thought occurred to him that he had more to give, that perhaps he had misjudged his worth. As his hope for the future took solid root, Paul's self-esteem rapidly improved. His newfound faith in himself generated an assurance that he had never before known. While just in its infancy, his emerging self-confidence became the foundation for an independent life.

Paul was still perplexed about what he wanted to do with his life. He knew that working in the laundry, while an important opportunity on which to build, was not the vehicle to drive him to his dreams. He had wanted to become a teacher at one time. "I still do," he says. "Maybe someday in some way, shape, or form, I'll be able to teach." Paul realizes that education should be a lifetime pursuit. He knows that there is no statute of limitation on a person's ability to learn.

Paul was introduced to the BOOST program at the time he found himself in this rejuvenated mode. He saw the chance to upgrade some of his skills and make himself more marketable. He made a commitment to go to BOOST class in the morning while working fulltime at the hotel at night. "I was pretty focused at the time because I really wanted to make something in my life work," he says.

His focus paid dividends. Paul completed the BOOST program, particularly enjoying the computer curriculum. "I've always liked computers because I can adapt to them well," he says. "I understand the theories behind them and I know what's going on. My hardest challenge with the computer is typing, because I have to type with one hand."

Lack of dexterity in his left hand has caused Paul to regularly consider his plight, should something happen to his right hand. "I'll just learn to adapt," he has determined. "I mean I would find ways. Other people have, so why not me?"

Graduation from BOOST brought with it a feeling of achievement and elation that Paul had very seldom felt. He had done his best and had been recognized for his accomplishment. He stood trembling to deliver his graduation speech, beads of perspiration cascading down his face. His voice was barely audible as he thanked those who had meant so much to him. While public speaking was not his greatest strength, his message was heart-felt and full of resolve to be the best person he could be. He now recognized that he had ability and value. Paul had experienced a renewal of self-esteem that produced the confidence he needed to tackle the world.

He was also confronted with the reality of saying goodbye to his classmates whose life experiences had taught him so much about drive, tenacity, and love. He was sad to see them go their separate ways but he knew that their relationships would endure the test of time and miles. The prospect that he might never see them again did not diminish the memories of their wonderful bonding that he would carry for a lifetime.

Within a matter of weeks, Paul was offered the first of several jobs at Discover Card. He started part time in the mailroom and then moved to a full-time position with benefits in the security department. The interview for the security position was another benchmark in the transformation of this great young man. "It was actually one of the first times in my life that I wasn't nervous talking to another person," Paul remembers. "No butterflies and I wasn't sweating profusely. I felt I had made a pretty good overview of myself. I left feeling that if I didn't get it, that's fine. I had put in my best effort."

The transformation was picking up momentum. "Can't" was replaced with "can," insecurity with confidence, rejection with acceptance, dependence with autonomy. In addition to his new position in security, he continued to work part time at the hotel until his financial life had been stabilized so he could support himself and his newly found independence.

Paul doesn't have a lot of new dreams; his original dream to have a wife and kids is still paramount in his life. He has already reached the objective of supporting himself and surviving on his own, a possibility that had almost vanished from reality just a few years ago. "My theory of life is that it always comes in steps," Paul is quick to point out. "Always in steps or building blocks. Whether you go straight up or around the bend, around an obstacle or over the clouds, you never stop trying."

This young man who as a child would shout at himself, "Why is this happening? Why am I even here?" has transformed into a compassionate volunteer who knows that he wasn't much use to others when he felt insecure about himself. "I want to help other people who haven't learned yet how to help themselves" is now Paul Murphy's rallying cry. The scrawny, withdrawn youth who caused such heartache to loving parents by attempting to take his own life has completed a marvelous transformation into a buff, athletic, articulate adult. He doesn't hide behind his imperfections. Indeed, he uses them to make himself stronger.

The former terrified speaker with such good things to say is now invited into the BOOST classroom to share his personal experience with other program participants, not to glorify himself, but to encourage those whose lives have been invaded by adversity. "Keep your dreams in front of you," he counsels them. "Never lose sight of what you really want because you have value and an important contribution to make."

Paul wants to help kids with disabilities. He believes that his personal experience can serve as an example to them. "There are things we can't grasp when we are young," he believes. "We don't know why some things happen to us, but we can control how we respond to the challenge."

A modern theory of psychology suggests that the body can achieve whatever the mind can conceive. The conception of ideas creates the seed of achievement. If one cannot see them or visualize them or feel them or dream them, one cannot possibly achieve them. Paul understands that many of his yet unfulfilled dreams can be achieved through understanding, confidence, and perseverance. He knows without question that he has significant control over his own evolutionary journey through life.

But most importantly, he recognizes a valuable opportunity to share, by his own life story, the exhilarating process of personal transformation. Paul Murphy has finally found an incredible way to become a teacher.

Stella

*T*he warm summer weather had driven many of the neighbors outside as Stella Gray arrived home to face the daunting task of climbing the porch stairs. She wore a dress that revealed two less-than-perfect legs, one cut off just above the knee and the other just below. As she sat in her wheelchair pondering the predicament that she had so often conquered, a twinge of embarrassment swept over her. This was different. She had dressed up earlier to accompany her boyfriend and now had no way to protect her knees and maintain her modesty.

It seemed as if the entire neighborhood was in suspended animation while she surveyed the scene and examined her options. Her boyfriend was more than willing to carry her up the stairs, but that clearly violated Stella's personal vow of independence. Besides, she is not a small person. Why should he risk hurting his back when she was perfectly capable of crawling up that flight of stairs, a feat she had accomplished so many times before?

While neighbors passively watched, Stella dropped out of the wheelchair and dragged herself to the first step. The everyday stair-climbing event common to most people was an arduous journey for Stella Gray. She crawled from step to step, pulling her body up with her arms while supporting herself on her knees. "It seemed so easy before I lost that first kneecap," she thought to herself.

This trip made her self-conscious. "I don't think this is going to work," she told her boyfriend. Her knees became raw as she continued to slowly claw and fight her way to the landing at the front door. Life had become extremely complicated these past years since the surgeries began.

A caesarian section was performed to deliver her first son when Stella was 19 years old. That was the first of more than 30 surgeries she would experience in the next 15 years. The baby was born with three holes in his heart, requiring prompt action to get him delivered. Stella was told that her son would not live to see his first birthday. Talented health care professionals were able to perform open-heart surgery that saved the baby's life. He has lived a normal, active lifestyle since the early trauma.

Mom, on the other hand, was not so fortunate. She was diagnosed with gestational diabetes during the pregnancy. All of the tests proved negative after delivery, but she suffered a reoccurrence two years later during a second pregnancy. The doctors thought the problem had again resolved itself naturally when no trace was detected after her second son was born. In just a few short years, however, drastic measures were being taken to save Stella's life.

At 22 and a young, single mother of two with little means of support, Stella found herself immersed in the drug scene. A boyfriend on drugs had introduced her to this new lifestyle. Since she had the philosophy, "If you can't beat them, join them," natural social forces pulled her into the pit. After two years, Stella realized the gravity of her situation. She made a conscious decision to quit "cold turkey." She had two sons to raise and goals to accomplish in her life. There was no time to waste on this destructive drug habit she had developed.

Some might rationalize their personal behavior and blame it on events they don't control. Stella's father died when she was 12. Those years were difficult, but she does not excuse herself because her father died prematurely. Her mother remarried a good man who treated Stella and her two brothers like his own children. Stella's sense of personal responsibility, acquired as a child and teenager, has been a powerful influence in shaping her independent spirit.

Stella developed a strong commitment to her boys and worked hard for several years to provide a better life for them. One day, when she was 28 years old, she bumped her foot. Within three weeks her toes had turned totally black with gangrene. Her life-changing visit to the doctor confirmed her greatest fear: the toes on her right foot needed to be removed to limit the spread of the infection. The doctor wanted to schedule a future appointment at the hospital to perform the procedure, but Stella insisted that the operation be done immediately. She was concerned about the emotional trauma that everyone concerned would experience, made more acute by waiting even one additional day.

After her toes were amputated, Stella left the hospital with her life saved. Mortality seemed to take on a new perspective as she thought about her boys and their future as a family. Diabetes was officially confirmed as the source of the problem and Stella was placed on a heavy insulin regimen. She learned how to stuff tissues into her shoe so she could walk and even dance. Life went on quite naturally. She didn't even lose much of her balance, as she was told might happen.

The diabetes, however, was raging in her body and became very difficult to control. Five months after the first amputation, the rest of her right foot started to turn black from infection. Another operation was necessary. The doctor gave her the option of removing the foot directly above the ankle or just below the knee. Recognizing the pattern that was developing, Stella decided to have the more radical surgery to, hopefully, stem the tide once and for all. "I don't let things get me down," she says, "I'm just the type of person who says what is going to be is going to be and whatever it is, you have to make the best out of it."

Infection and poor circulation continued to be major problems. Stella went into the hospital dozens of times for different treatments and operations. She had multiple surgeries to install artificial arteries and to control infection with IV infusion of antibiotics. On one occasion, Stella had gone to the hospital late at night suffering with internal bleeding. Since she spent so much time at the hospital, most of the staff knew her well. Stella's warm, friendly personality created relationships with her health care givers that often paid valuable dividends. On this night, the word spread rapidly that "Stella is back." A nurse came into her room in the middle of the night to wake her and say hello. During their short conversation, Stella reached down to rub her leg. She was greeted with a huge pool of blood in the bed. An artificial artery that had previously been installed had become infected. So much blood had been lost that an emergency blood transfusion was needed to save her life.

"There were a few times I just felt I was cheated," Stella says. "I don't know why I felt that way. It just seemed that they can send a man to the moon but they can't save somebody's leg. It's a hard thing to understand."

After one six-week stay in the hospital for IV treatment of infection, Stella knew that something had to be done to change the process. Being gone from her boys for that long a period was causing her to be very depressed. She felt helpless as a mother, totally dependent on the system. Her firm resolve to work out another method was the catalyst for the installation of a "hickman," which is a tube that is placed in the main artery of the chest. It is surgically implanted and is good for about six months. As long as the system is regularly flushed out and the nozzle is kept clean, the hickman provides a vehicle to use IV drugs at home.

Stella learned how to introduce IV antibiotics into the hickman in the privacy and convenience of her own home. Hickmans have been installed in her chest many times. She carries permanent scars after their removal. "So many people said I couldn't learn to do it," she says. "But you never say you can't do it. It just depends on how much you want it." Stella wanted it badly enough that she has become self-sufficient in using the antibiotics. Every six months she enters the hospital to have another hickman implanted. The antibiotics are then sent home with her to be used in a regular procedure that Stella provides for herself.

Stella's own health is not her only challenge. "I have so much stuff going on in my life I have no time to feel sorry for myself," she explains. Stella and her mother lived together for many years until her mother went blind as a result of diabetes. Stella was no longer able to provide the required care. "My mother is a strong woman," Stella explains. "She had diabetes for a long time but never complained, so we didn't recognize the pain she was always suffering."

Her mother's blindness has created unhappiness and a feeling of futility for both mother and daughter. Before the onset of the blindness, Stella's mother was her rock-solid, primary support. She always encouraged with compassion but never through pity. She constantly provided much-needed positive reinforcement for Stella without feeling sorry for her daughter. She gave selflessly as a beacon of happiness in an otherwise deteriorating world. The roles are now reversed. Stella has become the giver. "I tell her, 'Mom, I am in this wheelchair but I'm not giving up. People get tired. I understand that. I am sure that I will have my day one day when I will be tired too. I am just not ready to get tired yet." Stella is frustrated that she cannot appropriately care for her mother due to her own physical limitations.

Stella's stepfather continued to live with her but was severely limited with Alzheimer's disease. She tenderly cared for him during his long, personal struggle until he passed away, leaving another significant void in her life.

An older sister suffers from multiple sclerosis. She lives on her own and can't get out of bed, yet she continues to raise her children as a single mom without a word of complaint. She is Stella's role model. "Sometimes when I feel sorry for myself, I think of my sister. It is hard to be sick or stay depressed when I think of what she is going through. She is so much stronger than I am."

Friends and family have been a wonderful source of strength for Stella Gray. They treat her with dignity and respect because of her thirst for independence. She doesn't want to be considered "different." She doesn't want to be pitied. Stella wants to live her life to the fullest and be a positive example for her boys. "I tell my kids all the time that they can do what they want to do. They have been through a lot. But just because they don't have a father in the home and their mother has no legs doesn't mean that it's all right to stay at home and collect welfare. I don't want that for them. I want them to know that if I can do it with no legs, they can do it with both their legs."

The boys are now teenagers. They have experienced all the normal growing-up pitfalls – and then some. The oldest son didn't talk much to his mom. He kept his feelings bottled up inside of him. While Stella knew that the boys were having some hard times, she had difficulty in getting them to share what they were thinking and feeling. Stella often had to keep in direct contact with the schools they attended to understand much of what was happening in their lives. In addition to being a teenager, the oldest boy was ashamed. He would push his mother around in the wheelchair until he saw someone he knew. Immediately, he would find a place to hide his face or escape so he wouldn't be recognized.

The younger son was just the opposite. "You are supposed to come with me to school today," he announced to his mom. "We are going to have lunch together and then you can take me home." Stella wasn't worried about how the kids would treat her, but what would be their response to Brandon, her son? The teacher had already let everyone in the class know that Stella had lost her legs. Everything went fine until lunchtime arrived. Brandon was pushing his mom down the hall toward the lunchroom when two boys rushed up and yelled, "Oh, Brandon, your mom ain't got no legs." Stella was devastated and began to cry. Her worst fear was that someone was going to say something that would hurt her son's feelings. "I'll just go back into the classroom and wait for you until lunch is over," she said to Brandon through her tears. "No way," he said. "To hell with them; you are going to eat with me." Then he proudly pushed the chair into the lunchroom where he and his mother enjoyed a great time together with the other kids and their moms.

Both boys are now doing well with their mother's disability. They understand that she is a unique person with unusual challenges. They aren't embarrassed to be with her in public. They not only accept the situation, they are proud of her and what she has accomplished. The boys are also sensitive to other people with disabilities. They become upset when those around them are insensitive. Their example has created a positive model for their friends to emulate. Stella's boys are well served by the inspirational example of self-sufficiency provided by their mother. They will break out of a potential dependency cycle into a life of productivity and service to others because they have a great teacher. And, she just happens to be their mom.

Stella often finds herself in social situations with people she doesn't know, whether it's on the street, at work, in a restaurant, or some other public place. Her philosophy is that people who are comfortable with themselves help make others around them feel comfortable. On occasion, she will notice someone who is staring at her. She would much prefer a direct question about what happened to her to the covert, stolen glances she sometimes senses. Parents will regularly chastise their children for asking Stella questions about her legs. Her response is to assure the parents that she's fine with the questions. Her answer is direct and to the point. "I have diabetes and the doctors had to amputate my legs." She will often tease the questioner, especially if it is an adult. "I got run over by a car and my legs got cut off," is one of her favorite stories.

At times, people she knows casually through work or church will take the initiative to push her wheelchair, often without even asking. Stella is quick to tell them, always with kindness, that she is comfortable propelling herself. If she feels tired or needs some assistance, she will ask for it. Otherwise, making her way in the chair is an important part of her independence. Her pet peeve is the person who approaches unannounced from behind and begins to push the chair without being invited. She understands that the wheelchair is just an inanimate object to most people, but to Stella, it is a part of her body. It is how she transports herself from one place to another. It is her legs. Most people don't understand that. They often play with the arms, handgrips, or other components of the chair. To Stella, this apparent harmless intrusion is really quite serious. "They aren't just playing with the chair, they are playing with me," she reminds.

One day, while walking her dog on the sidewalk, Stella noticed a lady approaching from the opposite direction with a dog on a leash. To avoid any confrontation between her own 115-pound rottweiler and the oncoming dog, Stella wrapped the leash around her hand and held on tightly. Her dog lunged at the other dog with amazing power and jerked Stella right out of the wheelchair. She was dragged for the good part of a block tumbling and sliding along behind the rottweiler. Her knees and elbows were badly scraped and her clothes were ripped and torn. While she admits to have been "messed all up," Stella was back out the very next day to walk the dog. She didn't stop doing what she wanted to do; she just found a way to do it a little differently.

Additional surgeries have left Stella with both legs amputated well above the knee. The gangrene and infection continue to progress. The life-saving solution is always the same: take a little bit more of the infected leg. The pain is intense, rarely easing for a welcome moment of relief. Through it all, Stella continues to concentrate on what is good in her life. She has learned to ignore the obstacles that are continually dropped in her path. "I just laugh at them now," she says. "I am a true believer that things are going to work out fine, so I just laugh at my problems and don't let them get to me too much."

After graduating from BOOST, Stella was very anxious to get a job. She needed work to support her boys and wanted to feel like she was making a quality contribution to society. A week or two following graduation, Stella went to the hospital to lose her left knee. She had been scheduled for a job interview at Discover Card during the same time period. When she had recovered enough to talk, Stella called from the ICU and was granted her job interview over the phone from her hospital bed. She was immediately hired and asked to report to the Operation Center for further training when she had completed her convalescence.

The job at Discover Card has become very important to

Stella. Her mouth forms into a broad smile when she says, "People just accepted me for being me." That is very important to her because Stella doesn't want people to see her as a disabled person, she just wants to be seen as a person, the person that she is. "I never, ever, and I have been here for awhile, I have never heard anybody snicker, stare, or laugh. I've never, ever heard it once in here," she is proud to report. "I feel like I really belong, that these people are truly my friends."

The future is less than crystal clear for Stella. A chronic battle to preserve her health and her life occupies an inordinate amount of her time and emotional resources. "My goal," she says, "is to live to see my kids grown up and able to take care of themselves. If something has to happen to me, I ask the Lord to let it happen after they are grown and able to care for themselves. So, I fight for them. That is why I get up. It seems like every time I get knocked down, I come up stronger."

Life, the poet counsels, is lived best one day at a time. There are few among us who understand the wealth of opportunity that exists in every daily seed. We often drag ourselves to work, through the humdrum of each 24-hour period, rationalizing that if it doesn't happen today, there is always tomorrow. Stella Gray understands the value of work and each precious new day. "Nobody could have told me that I would feel the way I feel about myself now," she says. "It feels so good to work and not just sit home."

On this new day, as she pauses for a moment on the landing at her front door, Stella looks back at the staircase she has just conquered. The ramp that has been installed makes the trip much easier. She feels a flush of optimism. "You know," she says to no one in particular, "I think this is really going to work."

Marette

Most of us wouldn't know how to live in a room without doors to the outside world. Our access to life's opportunities is inhibited only by our own decisions and personal motivation. We examine what alternatives are available and then open the appropriate door to start the journey. While it isn't always that simple, because we often need help to find the correct combination to the door we want opened, resources are readily available to provide assistance and direction.

Marette Monson lived in a room without doors. When she was 17 years old, she and her mother sat in the living room of a prospective employer. Marette had answered a newspaper ad for a nanny and was invited to come for an interview. A door had finally been opened to this talented young lady with cerebral palsy. She knew she could be successful at this job. She loved kids and had proven herself before.

Marette had wanted a job all of her life but dozens of doors had remained closed due to her disability. She had filled out more job applications than anyone she knew. Yet, all of her friends and siblings had jobs. They worked in fast food restaurants, libraries, amusement parks, offices, daycare, almost anything you could imagine. There had always been an excuse for not hiring Marette. Most of them, she knew, were bogus but what more could be done?

Marette knew that this job would be different. She had discussed with her mother the need to disclose her disability early in the interview. They mutually agreed that Marette should sell herself first and then talk about the cerebral palsy later. After all, no one could possibly recognize that she had a disability while she was sitting down. The interview went very well. The employer was impressed with Marette's ability and maturity. The lady basically told her she had the job. They talked about how she would get to work and when she would start. Marette could see a door opening that she had waited so long to find. She was finally going to get a real job!

After the interview had concluded, Marette informed the lady of her cerebral palsy. A dark gray pallor spread across the future employer's face. Her mouth twisted into a serious frown from the delightful smile that had grown during their conversation. She sat in silence for what seemed an eternity before asking, "Do you have many blackouts?" Marette calmly taught her that cerebral palsy does not cause blackouts and wouldn't limit at all her ability to care for the lady's children. The explanation seemed to be understood and Marette was told that she would be contacted soon.

No one ever called. Another door remained closed. Another opportunity lost. The room without doors continued to be Marette's domain. Was it because she lacked talent? Ability? Drive? Persistence? No, this was again a case of not what she lacked but what she had been born with. Marette knows that she is not just her cerebral palsy, even if most of the world defines her that way. She is a human being with goals, ambition, needs, and dreams. Marette's disability has shaped both the way the outside world perceives her and how, at times, she sees herself.

The roots of Marette's physical challenges are easily traced to her birth. Because she was born two and a half months premature, her lungs were not sufficiently developed to supply enough oxygen to her brain. As a result, some bleeding occurred which damaged the part of the brain that controls muscle relaxation in the legs, a mild form of cerebral palsy. The diagnosis was not made until she was 18 months old when her mother became concerned that she still couldn't walk, crawl, or even sit up by herself.

Marette had her first operation at age two and a half. Until then, her leg muscles were continually contracted, leaving them tight, twisted, and difficult to move. The doctor cut her heel cords, then stretched them so her feet were naturally flat on the ground. She was required to wear casts on both legs for six months. With great perseverance, Marette learned to walk with her knees bent inward, feet twisted toward each other.

Until she went to school, Marette didn't really notice that she was much different from the other kids. However, two sixth grade boys shattered her vision of normalcy on the first day of kindergarten when they mimicked the way she walked by contorting their legs into gross positions and made verbal fun of her as she walked to class. Marette was devastated. She burst into tears as she arrived home after school. "This isn't fair," she told her mom. "Why can't I walk right? Why are the kids so mean? There is nothing wrong with me."

The advice given by her mother became the standard by which Marette governed her early life. "Just ignore them," her mother suggested. "They are the ones with the problem; they are the ones who are ignorant." Her mother repeated the same counsel each time Marette returned home in tears. While ignoring the treatment she received did not make it go away, the technique allowed Marette to cope with the constant teasing.

Still, the hurt grew deep. At times, she felt her heart would shatter into little pieces. She was labeled as "different" and had no friends. Her constant question became, "Can I play with you?" And the regular response, "Maybe next time." But next time never came. Marette was left to wander the playground at recess asking but never being allowed to join in. Sometimes there were snickers; sometimes blatant teasing; always rejection. Marette was left to sit alone on a bench waiting for her chance to play, not really understanding why she was not allowed to be part of the society she so desperately wanted to join.

No more surgeries were performed for eight years. Marette's muscles continued to tighten until she was again walking on her toes. She adapted to the gradual deterioration, as children are capable of doing, and even learned how to run. At age 10, however, sharp pains developed in her hips and thighs. The pain became so intense that Marette often had to come home early from school.

Her parents consulted with the doctor. They were told that something had to be done in order to avoid hip dislocations and other serious problems. Marette did not want to continue a pattern of repeated operations to perform the same procedure, but she also wanted to avoid the complications associated with continual hip deterioration.

A new surgical procedure called rhizotomy had been developed to address the problem. An incision is made in the back. The nerves that are sending the signals to keep the muscles contracted are then severed. The best nerves are retained, obviously, since full paralysis would occur if they were all cut. Once the worst nerves are severed, the muscles relax. Since many of the affected muscles have been used sparingly, the patient must learn how to walk again.

Marette was excited to learn to use the muscles she had never used. She could envision her feet lying naturally flat, walking perfectly like her friends. While the risk of total paralysis was very real, Marette didn't consider the down side. This is what she had wanted her entire life and this surgery, she knew, would be the miracle cure.

The decision was made to proceed.

Only two doctors in the world were able to perform the procedure. One of them had his practice at Primary Children's Hospital in Salt Lake City. Marette was carefully evaluated, then approved for surgery. The operation went well but Marette was terrified when she woke up and couldn't move or even feel her legs. She thought they had made a terrible mistake. Even though she was confined to bed and a wheelchair during many months of hospital rehabilitation, the surgery had been successful. What faced her now was the daunting challenge of learning to walk again.

Marette also faced another significant challenge when she was told, while still in the hospital, that her parents were getting a divorce. It was the most awful time of her life. She was lying paralyzed in the hospital fighting to learn how to use her legs again and confronted with the reality of her parents' divorce. Her father also used Marette as a shoulder to cry on. The emotional and physical trauma affected her immensely. She lost her appetite and completely stopped eating. She was taken to see a psychologist but refused to talk. Life had changed dramatically for this 10-year old who had entered the hospital with such high expectations for a better life.

Meanwhile, the physical therapy was working well. With a determined spirit, Marette attacked the challenge of re-learning how to walk. She labored with great effort and slowly began to see some positive results. Ultimately, but for only a short time, she could walk almost perfectly. She thought the surgery had been the cure she so desperately wanted, but, as the years went by, the muscles

Marette had learned to use began to tighten again. She was devastated as she contemplated the future.

Maxims designed to stimulate and motivate the human spirit became very negative for Marette as she struggled to overcome her cerebral palsy. "You can do anything you want if you just put your mind to it," was the rallying cry. "You can be anything you want to be," shouted the prevailing wisdom. Marette gradually became aware that many of those doors were closed to her. She could never become an Olympic sprinter. She would never even be able to run and jump like her friends.

Her father reinforced the unrealistic expectations. He wanted desperately for Marette to be "normal." Unfortunately, she always suspected his motive. She felt that he was embarrassed by her. While his involvement was commendable, his reinforcement was never positive. He didn't congratulate her when she was doing well, he told her she should do better. "We can beat this thing," was his motto. The constant prodding created a deep chasm between them. Marette grew weary of his questionable motivation.

Swimming became an important part of her therapy as muscles continued to tighten through the early teenage years. Marette's father, who was now divorced from her mother, would come to take Marette swimming each week. He decided that if once was good, two times a week was twice as good. After a conversation with her sister, Marette realized how misplaced the expectation was. She had cerebral palsy. There was no cure! Her father was being unfair to expect her to " become normal."

The need for another surgery had already been indicated by the time Marette was 14. She realized that the four years she had spent vigorously exercising and trying to get better were not going to change the fact that she needed another operation. "This is brain damage," she told herself, "No matter how many times I go swimming, it is not going to go away." Her hamstrings were stretched in two surgeries a year apart.

A haunting gap widened between Marette and her father until his death a few years later. "I don't think my dad was proud of me," she says. "He never told me that he was. He never acted like he was. Every time I did something good, it never was good enough."

Marette attended three different high schools. There were some isolated unfortunate incidents, but her life at school was generally happy. It was during this time that Marette learned an important lesson about being different. "When you run into a situation or you are having a hard time or you feel bad," she says, "there are two things that you can do. One, you can feel sorry for yourself and give up and say fine, I'm not even going to try. Or you can do something about it." She learned how to stand up for herself and also for others. The principle of "ignoring" that she used so effectively as a child no longer served her well.

Marette realized that the preoccupation with physical appearance so prevalent in our society is not attainable for many people with disabilities. In fact, obsessive dieting, excessive workouts, and mysterious plastic surgery don't make sports heroes, models, or beauty queens out of most people. While Marette was seduced into the belief of physical perfection for a time, she soon learned who she was and what she could contribute. She realized that she had talents and potential. Her decision was to be the best person that she could be.

As Marette began to set realistic goals, she ended the debilitating exercise of setting herself up for failure. Instead of focusing on what she wasn't, Marette decided to focus on what she was. She still sits on the sidelines and wonders what it feels like to have the wind blowing in your face as you run; what it would be like to walk in the dark without falling; or what it's like to bend your toes or feel your feet. She still senses the silent stares of people in the supermarket. She still wonders if her own story of triumph over enormous odds could ever have compared to the life of Glen Cunningham, the Olympic champion runner who was badly burned as a child, or Rena, the blind girl who was able to regain her sight after a miraculous surgery.

The great transformation that took place was internal. It was not in how others viewed Marette, but in how Marette viewed herself. Society had not changed its image of the disabled; Marette had changed hers. The negative impacts of cerebral palsy are still present. Those things, however, in no way compare to what Marette feels she has learned because of her disability.

Some windows started to appear in her room without doors. Still, she felt restricted from actively participating in the world she could visualize, especially after repeated attempts to find employment. Her mother's positive example taught Marette the value of a college education: After the divorce, her mother had gone back to college. She shouldered the responsibility of raising her family with some public assistance while she pursued a degree. Marette wanted to emulate her mother's example but realized she had to find a job to make her dream become a reality.

Every possible avenue was explored. Employers were simply not willing to give Marette a chance to prove herself. She was rejected out of hand because of her cerebral palsy. She became discouraged as she attempted to open every door she could think of. None would open. She didn't have the right combination. Attempts were made to access numerous government programs but each road resulted in a dead end. No one seemed to want to help. She found little encouragement outside of her mother and family, especially from those who are charged with opening doors for people with special needs.

She was constantly greeted with rejection and disapproval. All she wanted was an opportunity. Why was this so difficult? She was intelligent, talented, and motivated. Someone must need an employee like that! One government worker even suggested that Marette just give up the search for a job because she had exhausted all her possibilities. So what was the alternative? Social Security for life? The public dole? No, these were not options for a person who had so much to give.

Almost by chance, Marette was given a limited recommendation about the BOOST program by a social worker. Marette was very cynical by this time about any so-called "program." However, as she had done so many times before, Marette followed up by introducing herself to the BOOST recruiters. Within a short time, she was matriculated into a BOOST class. Her initial understanding was that BOOST was focused at business skills. That wasn't really the direction she wanted to pursue. Rather, she wanted to become a social worker to help others negotiate the systems she had found so difficult for herself. Nevertheless, she worked hard in BOOST and learned some important skills that would serve her well in her pursuit of meaningful employment.

After completing the class, Marette was encouraged by the people at Discover Card to apply for a job. The rest, as they say, is history. She went to work in loss prevention. Marette likes to say, "I don't collect bills, I give people an opportunity to fulfill their obligations." Her performance was so outstanding that she quickly received promotions and pay increases.

She enrolled at Brigham Young University to pursue her college education dream while continuing to work at Discover Card on a part-time basis. Her honors and recognition were record setting. She was recognized several times as an "Excellence" winner in her Operations Center. Later, Marette was awarded the prestigious "Pinnacle of Excellence" award given nationally to the most elite Discover Card employees. Even though working just part time, she was invited to be a coach, a position reserved exclusively for full-time employees.

After graduating from BYU with high honors, Marette was

accepted into the graduate program of social work at the University of Utah, where her academic achievement continued to reach superior levels. During her graduate schooling, Marette also continued her work at Discover Card with one significant change: She was selected to be the full-time BOOST Coordinator at the Lake Park Operations Center in Utah.

"I look at all of those other people who didn't give me a chance and I think, you missed out," Marette says. "Discover Card was the only one who gave me a chance and look what a good employee they got. A chance doesn't seem like that much to ask."

Marette is a very articulate young woman. She now knows who she is and how she is going to achieve her goals in life. Marette is also passionate about helping others recognize their full potential, having become a tireless community voice for people with physical disabilities. "We are just like everyone else," Marette is quick to point out, "and just like everyone else deserves a chance, so do we. Remember not to put unrealistic expectations on us and love us for who we are. Don't try to change us into something we are not."

There are so many who believe they live in rooms without doors. When opportunity and hope are lost, the human spirit suffers serious atrophy. Independence defaults to dependency; strength deteriorates into weakness; talent is dissipated; potential is wasted. Tenacity and perseverance cannot long survive alone in a vacuum; a helping hand from someone who cares must sustain them.

Marette Monson cares! She cares about making the best of what she has. She cares about having a chance for herself. But most of all, she cares about using her experience to identify and unlock doors of opportunity for those who believe they do not exist.

Susan C.

Everything was right with the world . . . or so it seemed on the surface of this peaceful scene. Susan Conard was doing what she loved to do most. Whenever she rode her horse with gusto through the warm California countryside, everyday cares would melt away like soft serve ice cream. The refreshing breeze that rushed past her head temporarily dislodged the feelings of inadequacy and inferior self-esteem that had dogged her for most of her young life.

She was just 12 years old, but in the tranquility of moments like these, Susan had already discovered a refuge from the mean-spirited circumstances that had engulfed her. As rider and horse paused for a much-needed break, reality jolted her 230-pound frame in the form of yet another derogatory comment. "Get off and let the horse ride awhile," yelled a group of boys standing near the fence. They laughed heartily at Susan's expense, probably not even recognizing the awful intrusion they had made into her only sanctuary.

Susan's weight had created havoc with her self-esteem. She was an extreme introvert, feeling very uncomfortable around people, including her own family. "I didn't feel I was good enough," Susan remembers. While working in the family print shop business as a young girl, her feeling of bankrupt self-worth was again badly hammered. Susan and her sisters had an assignment to pick up and deliver the printing jobs each afternoon. "I knew there were times they didn't want to take me," she recalls. "Or, they would take me but they would tell me to stay in the car and my sisters would go in. I assumed it was because they were ashamed of me because of my weight."

No one in Susan's family had a serious weight problem. Her mother and father, as well as her sisters, were all a little overweight, but none was obese. Her parents were concerned about the health issues as well as the social consequences, so Susan was taken to a weight doctor, who started her on diet pills at the age of eight. Her young body aggressively rebelled. She felt like a war was being waged inside her. The "upper" sensation that was created caused a terrible nervous response. Doctors became her enemy. Depression initiated its long, slowly advancing trespass into her life.

As a pre-teen, Susan even struggled with her relationship with a grandmother whom she idolized. An older sister was greatly favored to the point that she had a room in grandma's next-door house. Susan, on the other hand, felt ignored and isolated. Finally, with Susan in her teens, the normal adolescent vulnerabilities, and additional exposure to drugs, Susan's grandmother began to reach out in an act of protection. Being suddenly included rekindled significant cynicism for a guarded young woman. She recognized the attempt as a "feel-good" gesture for grandma as much as an honest statement of love.

Grandma did make an attempt to reinforce Susan's self-image later in life. She often commented to her granddaughter, "You have such a wonderful personality; people love to be around you. You just have that talent."

During the difficult high school years, Susan's academic achievement was the only consistent esteem builder in her life. She was smart and did well with her studies. However, the social environment at school caused Susan to feel highly threatened. She knew she was different! Going to school became an obstacle that she often did not conquer. While living in California, Susan was particularly successful with her schoolwork because of the emphasis on getting the work done and scoring well on tests. Her sporadic attendance did not adversely affect her grades. After moving to Oregon, where attendance counted toward the grade, Susan's success plummeted. She achieved the highest score on a midterm test in a business class but received a D- because of her poor attendance.

The system did not serve Susan well. Her public education became a trial of her ability to overcome the social embarrassment

created by her weight, rather than a test of her academic achievement. She felt ostracized and lonely. A consensus decision was
reached that Susan would permanently leave school. Because she
was not yet 18, her parents were required to sign for her. They
agreed after establishing the stipulation that she would pass the
GED and immediately start college.

 While the rest of her schoolmates were laboring through
their senior year of high school, Susan easily completed the GED
requirements for graduation and began college right after the first
of the year. The college course catalog was a maze to her as she
researched the classes. She knew nothing of upper or lower division courses and no one in her family knew how to guide her. The
process became entangled as Susan blindly enrolled in courses that
were significantly beyond her reach. By mustering the maximum
courage she possessed, Susan temporarily overcame the fear and
began her college career, only to find that she had totally messed
up her schedule. She was crushed. Another blow landed squarely
on a delicate self-image. Her depression deepened, roots strengthening with each new rejection or failure.

 The time had come for Susan to find a job outside the family printing business. Since she had worked from the age of five
doing hand collating and other chores, a job at a large printing
plant was not difficult to acquire. Actually beginning the job and
forging relationships with other employees, however, was a major
obstacle. The situation was extremely awkward, at best, but soon
Susan's skills began to be recognized by her peers. She was good at

what she did. Supervisors and co-workers were amazed at her speed and accuracy.

As Susan's professional expertise became acknowledged, her sense of worth started to improve. She found in her peers at work a group of people who were non-threatening to her. They became her friends. They included her in their activities. She found herself laughing at their jokes. Up to this time, she could barely manage a smile, rarely feeling that anything was very humorous. People throughout her life had regularly told her, "You never laugh at anything."

A positive transformation began. Not only did Susan learn to laugh, she also learned to open up. This was a fun crowd. She enjoyed them. She loved going to work. A promotion to shipping clerk was offered and accepted. Susan had finally, after more than 18 years, turned her life in a positive direction. She felt good about herself and the contribution she was making. She felt accepted and rewarded. Nothing could stop her now!

The promise of some blue sky in a heretofore mostly cloudy life was short lived. Soon after taking the job as a shipping clerk, Susan injured her back. The job at the printing company, including the wonderful therapeutic effect it was having on her self-image, collapsed in an instant. She felt like a human dummy in an automobile crash test. "I felt like my world had come to an end," Susan painfully remembers.

A disability evaluation center was the next stop. For six weeks, Susan was evaluated, psychoanalyzed, tested, and provided with physical and occupational therapy on an in-patient basis. She hated the experience. Overdosing on painkillers became her way of making a passionate plea for help. But no overt reaction was going to change the fact that a congenital back defect, aggravated by her weight, had been uncovered. Susan was told that she could never go back to the type of work that had produced her few moments of true happiness.

The prescribed solution was "return to college," a prospect that petrified this disillusioned young woman. Images of loneliness, lack of acceptance, and self-questioning of her ability produced great anxiety. The fears she visualized were soon realized.

Since the vocational testing that had been done was relatively inconclusive, Susan made a hesitant decision to pursue the graphic arts, a field allied with her past comfortable work experience. A move to Portland, Oregon was required in order to begin her schooling. She was homesick, frightened, and terribly lonely. The isolation produced by having no friends, or even a phone, resulted in a return to her previously diagnosed suicidal tendencies.

During this rough period, Susan returned home for a few days to have a plate removed from a leg she had previously broken. Upon returning to Portland, her elderly landlady's memory had taken a turn for the worse. She didn't even recognize Susan. The arrangement they had negotiated for Susan to care for the lady in exchange for board and room was abruptly terminated. Since her finances were limited, Susan was again confronted with a serious threat to her stability. She had no place to live.

Members of her church came to the rescue and found a room in the home of an elderly couple. Susan got involved in church activities and was given the assignment to be in charge of the sports program for the young women. To begin with, only four girls were attending on a regular basis. By the time she left the area, 21 girls were actively participating.

Susan loved that experience. She learned to give of herself and recognized the positive contribution she was making to the lives of those young women. She developed a strong desire to continue her education; social life didn't seem to matter anymore. A night job allowed her to earn enough money to go back to school. She became successful, even getting A's in chemistry and math. Life was picking up some positive momentum for Susan Conard.

A move by her parents to Salt Lake City prompted Susan to make the move as well. Many factors combined to restrict her from pursuing her education at that time, but positive work experiences continued to support the emerging self-confidence that she felt. Still very heavy and self-conscious, Susan was pleased to learn that she was eligible to serve a mission for her church, a life-long dream she had quietly maintained. She had assumed that because she was substantially overweight, the opportunity to go on a mission was not available to her.

Two months later she was in England. The mission experience reinforced her feeling of self-worth. "I loved the people; I loved the work," Susan says. She was very successful. Through her ability to love without judgment, she taught everyone she met a wonderful lesson. Her example was her sermon. Her mission president publicly recognized her as "one of the finest people he had ever worked with." He went on to say, "It is her attitude that makes the difference."

Strain on Susan's back from the walking and vigorous physical effort ultimately cut short the 18-month mission to just over a year. Even though everyone agreed with the decision, returning home without fulfilling the entire commitment caused emotional pain. Successful reality was replaced again with perceived failure and rejection. To add to the psychological challenges she was facing, her back pain quickly dissipated when she arrived home to the dryer climate. Susan began to question herself, "Was it all in my head?" The delicate mental balance she had nursed into health over the past several years was again in serious jeopardy.

Shortly after arriving home, Susan was reintroduced to Bruce, a friend she had spent time with in Oregon. He had moved to Salt Lake while she was in England. They decided that neither was looking for a permanent relationship but within a month Bruce asked Susan to marry him. She was unsure. He was a good, compassionate man but he had pretty much given up on himself. He had been treated like he was "retarded" most of his life due to a speech impediment that 19 major operations had not significantly helped.

Susan was attracted to his goodness. She knew he was the type of person that would do anything to help someone in need. Her parents were not happy with her decision to marry him, especially her mother. Those months were very difficult for Susan as she prepared for her marriage. She attempted to build bridges to those who questioned her decision, while continuing to wrestle with her own private demons.

Within the first year of marriage, Susan had her first child. She was also working two or three jobs trying to keep the family financial ship afloat because Bruce had been laid off work. One of her jobs was with a publishing company. Susan noticed that the company outsourced the typesetting on about half of the books they published. "Why couldn't I do that at home?" she asked herself. The answer was a resounding "Why not?"

There were, of course, significant obstacles to overcome, not the least of which being the acquisition of expensive equipment. Most of the feedback to her idea was negative. Susan's father was a typesetter himself and very skeptical about the venture. He, and other members of the family, didn't think she could make it in business by herself. Nevertheless, Susan felt strongly that this new enterprise would provide her with the opportunity to be home with her children and still contribute much-needed financial support. The decision was made to move forward by acquiring a sizable loan to buy the equipment.

Susan's expectation was to reduce her 60 to 80-hour workweeks to a couple of 12-hour days a week at home doing typesetting. The business venture began with promise, continuing to move toward achievement of its goals. While business improved at a steady pace, Susan's stress increased at a much faster rate. She gave birth to a third child during this time and almost died during the delivery. Her blood pressure reached 220/190.

In one calendar year, Susan had her gall bladder removed, watched her brother-in-law die, grieved with her business partner who lost a baby late in the pregnancy, and checked herself into a pain clinic to learn how to manage pain without drugs. She had been relying on excessive daily doses of Percodan to control her intense back pain – and she began to like the way it made her feel. All this time her weight continued to balloon.

A psychotherapist, in collaboration with her social worker, put Susan under hypnosis in an effort to unlock the source of her problems. Upon awaking from the hypnosis, Susan became aggressively suicidal. She was committed to a mental hospital for treatment. For the next four years, she was in and out of mental health facilities dozens of times. Her entrepreneurial dream became a wistful memory. The financial crisis created by her inability to work and pay off the balance on the typesetting equipment grew more acute each day.

Her self-image dropped like a rock thrown into a deep canyon. "I tried to kill myself," Susan says. "I thought my only worth to my family was financial and that was cut off." After a conversation with a social worker who suggested applying for government financial assistance, Susan became despondent. "I did what I always did," she says. "I could think of nothing but razor blades." She was quickly committed once again to a hospital. That night she attempted suicide once again. "I wasn't even capable of doing that right," she declares.

The hospital staff was rude to Susan because one of their peers, who had conducted the strip search at check-in, had been reprimanded for not uncovering the blades. Her hands were roughly bandaged and enclosed in large mittens. Susan was put into isolation, draped only with a tiny gown that did not cover her large frame. She was humiliated. The next morning she was served breakfast on a bare tray with no utensils. The nurse caustically chided her by saying, "It's kinda' hard that way, huh?"

No visitors were allowed. Susan was left alone to deal with the embarrassment of removing her gown each night while the staff searched her entire body. The humiliation caused enormous psychological damage.

There was no air conditioning in the room; the heat became unbearable, often reaching temperatures of over 100°F. She was moved into a room with six occupied beds. The other patients were extremely angry, some to the point of violence. Most used crude and abusive language that was offensive to Susan. She was here to get help but felt that the treatment, particularly the environment of the facility, was far worse than the disease.

Susan was taught to take gradual steps in her rehabilitation. The process worked to the extent that she was able to function outside of the hospital setting. A portion of the real world reluctantly welcomed her but the resumption of employment totally evaded her grasp. Her father responded to an evaluation by the Social Security Administration by saying, "You don't understand my daughter. She really loves to work but she can't even help me here at the print shop. She is basically non-functional."

Financial needs were acute, with nowhere to turn. A vocational rehabilitation counselor suggested that Susan investigate the BOOST program. Having been to college for a couple of years, she didn't understand how a program like this could possibly supplement her skills sufficiently to make any difference. Her apprehension quickly evaporated. "Once I walked into the class, I felt accepted," Susan says. "I felt normal; I felt understood. No one seemed to be judging me."

The thought of learning how to use a computer with a mouse and smart icons produced additional anguish for Susan. She was concerned about her ability to learn something new, especially considering her past fears and experience. Again, the extreme emotional crisis was short-lived. Not only did Susan quickly learn the new technology, but also became a great support for others in the class who had never used a computer and were afraid to try. The positive strokes she received for her own success, coupled with the sincere appreciation expressed by her classmates, fed her socialization need for the first time in years. A sense of worthlessness was replaced with a warm feeling of being valued. It wasn't so much how she looked to these people, but what she did.

An experience during her BOOST class strengthened Susan's emerging sense of personal value. One of the facilitators whispered to her, "I hear you have Discover Card potential." The thought of actually working again terrified Susan but the fact that someone she highly respected recognized her potential was a huge stroke. Since her anxiety level remained very high, Susan was asked to help with the BOOST program for a while rather than jump with both feet into a full-time job. "I was offered the opportunity to tutor the next two classes and that was a little scary," she says. "But I loved it. I loved it so much. It was amazing. I looked forward to every day of tutoring."

The anxiety disorder that Susan deals with every day caused a continued struggle to maintain her weight. The day Susan interviewed for BOOST she weighed 330 pounds. Her weight later increased about 20 pounds due to a constant battle with plantar warts in her foot that make exercise very difficult. At times, she suffered emotional paralysis to the point of not being able to even get out of bed.

Through it all, Susan continued her role as a successful BOOST tutor. Those who have felt the influence of her patient coaching honor Susan by their expressions of sincere appreciation. They know she cares about them so they return her warmth and love. "It's something that you feel comfortable with," Susan explains, "something you are contributing to and that you are good at. All of those things make you feel good."

The personal comfort zone Susan discovered at BOOST helped her become a solid support for her peers. "I didn't feel like an oddball in the classes," she says. Perhaps that is why she recommended that her husband, Bruce, enroll in BOOST. After successfully completing the program, Bruce found quality, long-term employment at the University of Utah. He is proud of his wife. He saw the way the BOOST participants responded to her and heard the positive things they said about her. Bruce knows that she makes an important difference in their lives. "They love you," he continually reminds her.

Susan is the epitome of selfless service performed in the shadows, not recognized or appreciated by anyone beyond those lucky enough to be touched by her compassionate heart. When a BOOST class was organized at a new building in an area of the city not yet served by public transportation, Susan made the commitment to travel dozens of miles out of her way every day to pick up five participants who had no way to get to and from class. She did this on her own initiative, without remuneration or public fanfare. Although she wrestles with her own silent and invisible demons, Susan continues to give of herself to lighten the burdens of those around her.

Supported by modern surgical procedures, Susan has been able to lose more than 100 pounds. She feels better about herself, using her renewed self-confidence to assume a full-time job at Discover Card. Her pleasant demeanor and fun personality have come to the surface.

Still, Susan's anxiety levels remain high in many situations. She struggles to find a sanctuary similar to that of her youth, a place to escape the foreboding nightmare that often engulfs her. How she longs for the temporary relief she was afforded by riding her faithful horse through a peaceful countryside! Though no longer faced so much with the derogatory catcalls of immature boys, Susan wages a courageous battle every day of her life just to live in a world in which she feels she does not fit.

Most of us do not fully comprehend the debilitating effects of depression and mental illness. We tend to understand them as personal choices rather than disabilities. We often perceive those who are incapacitated by psychological challenges as weak or irresponsible. When these situations are viewed up close, however, the perspective changes considerably. Those like Susan Conard, whose lives are darkened by such circumstances, teach us by their courage in the face of hopelessness. Ultimately, by being responsive to the lessons, we will experience the far greater growth.

Joel

—— •∷═•●◑◐●•═∷• ——

wenty-five eye surgeries in a little over four years would create a significant level of apprehension and frustration at any time during life. Starting your life with that level of trauma raises the challenge to an entirely different level.

Joel Bonnecarre was born with glaucoma, a debilitating eye disease that is caused by pressure in the retina. Between the ages of eight months and five years, he had 25 operations to relieve pressure and improve his chances to be normally sighted. The pain was often so intense that this otherwise glib, talkative child was reduced to an almost catatonic state just trying to deal with the awful distress.

The pain germinates from swelling in the retina that, in turn, causes pressure on the brain and ultimately extreme

headaches. Joel remembers little about those days of terrible discomfort, except the intense, debilitating pain. Along with the pain,
of course, was the problem of deteriorating vision. He was later
told that he has one of the worst cases of survivable glaucoma that
the medical community has ever seen.

A loving, supportive family was a great blessing to this vul-
nerable little boy who was fighting so hard to find that comfortable
place where he could simply be a kid. His family, however, was
very protective of what they perceived to be their fragile child and
brother. Joel understands that now. At five, he became very frustrated with it all. "I had to fight to even go outside," Joel remembers. "They wouldn't even let me go out the door unsupervised,
and we lived in a quiet neighborhood."

Joel wanted to run and play with the other kids. He wanted
the chance to be like them. He felt like a prisoner in his own
home. Not only did he suffer from low vision and the associated
pain, he was restricted from growing up normally, to really experience life as a child.

Because Joel's siblings were all much older than he, the isolation that he felt was intensified. They had their adolescent and
young adult lives to lead while Joel sat home with nothing to do.
Friendships are always important in life, but the bond that was
forged between six-year-old Joel and his newfound friend, four-
year-old Ray, created a very important contact with the emerging
world. They became best friends. Decades later, their friendship
and mutual admiration continue to flourish even though they live

in different parts of the country.

Joel attended the Louisiana School for the Visually Impaired during his entire public school career. It was a hard school. The core subjects like math, science, and English were especially difficult at the beginning. Teachers expected a lot from their blind and visually impaired students because they wanted to prepare these young people for the realities of adult life in a sighted world.

From the numerous early surgeries until age 10, Joel's vision remained about the same. He could see relatively well, especially considering what the possible outcome might have been. Then, at age 10, he suffered a setback. His vision was reduced perceptibly but stabilized with little deterioration for the next eight or nine years. Joel could see LCD illuminated readouts and could read larger block print. He could also walk pretty much wherever he wanted without the use of a cane.

Joel didn't consider his teenage years to be particularly unusual. "You know, the life of a blind person is not that much different from the life of a sighted person," he opines. "God puts different tasks on us all that are different from anyone else. He wants to make sure that we all have an even row. While the challenges are similar in harshness, they are not the same."

Because of Joel's determination to escape the sheltered life he knew as a blind child, he chose friends who were sighted. It was a conscious decision that he made because he didn't want to feel like he was kept in the perceived "prison" he remembered from his youth. He became just "one of the guys" with many of his friends until the mid-teenage years when his buddies started to drive. They became more mobile than he. Parties and functions were easy for them to attend because they merely jumped in a car and drove to the fun.

Joel, on the other hand, was very limited. He had to rely on his dad to take him and pick him up, a social gaffe that separated Joel from his friends. Having your dad tag along with you was not really accepted in the high school social scene. Since he didn't want to be labeled as a misfit, Joel made the decision to stay away from most of the functions. He didn't think it was very fair at the time but grew to realize how unimportant it all was in the big picture of life.

At the Louisiana School for the Visually Impaired, Joel learned how to wrestle. Most of us have difficulty comprehending how a blind person could possibly wrestle without clearly seeing the opponent. However, blind and visually impaired competitors participate in constant contact wrestling. Instead of starting in the traditional crouched position, constant contact wrestlers begin with hands touching. They never break contact with the opponent throughout the match and are thereby able to compete.

Joel learned some important life-lessons from his wrestling experience. "A successful wrestling team is not just made up of a bunch of good wrestlers," Joel suggests. "While it is full of good wrestlers, it's also full of people who support one another. They not only cheer for you while you are wrestling, they're cheering and helping you off the mat as well." The struggle for independence that Joel had waged throughout his young life took on some additional meaning as he began to understand that everyone needs a helping hand. Everyone needs support. Everyone needs someone to cheer for them.

Rising to tenth in his weight class in the Louisiana State rankings, Joel was proud of his accomplishments. However, 12 shoulder separations in one year dampened his enthusiasm. There was no money to surgically repair the damage, so Joel dropped out of wrestling. It was during this time that he also developed a close personal attachment to long hair. Since long hair was not allowed on the wrestling team, the decision to quit became even more timely.

Long hair did fit nicely with music, his other love. Joel grew up in a household of excellent musicians. From the time he was a baby, Joel's older brothers stroked his affinity for music by sitting him in his stroller while they practiced the guitar, piano, and saxophone. As he got older, Joel displayed an amazing ability to play a number of musical instruments. He also developed a good singing voice. Piano, lead guitar, and bass guitar became his instruments of choice as he embarked on an exciting music career that also brought him into contact with some of his greatest personal challenges.

Learning to play the guitar was facilitated by a guitar teacher who preferred an "ear reader" to a "sight reader." Although Joel had studied and was able to read Braille music, he was encouraged by his teacher, a world-renowned guitarist, who saw him as an artist, not a musical mechanic. They worked together to enhance Joel's natural ability to anticipate where the music is going. Instead of reading music like a machine, Joel was able to feel the passages and understand what they meant. His musical senses became so refined that he could almost taste the subtleties.

Hundreds of hours of practice and hard work fed his passion for music. It became more than just a hobby. Music became Joel's life and profession. He became frustrated with the cavalier attitude of friends, family, and even other musicians who saw music as a terrific hobby, but certainly not a way to make a living. Joel practiced eight or ten hours a day, sometimes until his fingers would bleed. His musical zeal transformed him into a perfectionist. He became insulted when others would not take seriously his powerful commitment to be the best musician that he could possibly be. "They just didn't understand," Joel says. "I've put a huge amount of work into my music. It is not senseless, it is my passion."

Other dynamics were raging in Joel's life during the days of his emerging musical obsession. A bipolar disorder caused him to fluctuate between excessive enthusiasm and deep depression. Because the psychological diagnosis was not made for many years, Joel was not aware of what was happening to him; teachers labeled him as lazy and spoiled. He graduated from school with the narrowest tolerance. He considered his graduation to be a gift, an adjustment of the standards to allow him, and others in his class, to get the diploma so they would have a better chance at life. Joel looks at that experience now as an easy way out rather than a good foundation for life.

Joel's manic-depressive illness became even more intense

when his vision began to regress. He would lash out at people for no apparent reason. His aggressive, unpredictable behavior left him without friends.

His father and medical experts had told him that his glaucoma could ultimately cause him to go totally blind. Joel perceived himself to be legally blind, but he was certainly not totally blind. There was a big difference in his mind between the two. Facing the imminent prospect of total blindness was not easy, though he had been warned all of his life. Joel reminisces, "It's really easy if you're an outsider to say, 'Well, you've been told all your life that this was going to happen.' But when it happens, it's a different story."

Another surgery was performed when Joel was 21. Later, a shunt was put into one eye to drain the fluid off the retina. These, and other procedures, helped to stabilize the deteriorating situation, although Joel almost completely lost his vision.

A move to Phoenix, Arizona was precipitated by Joel's continued attraction to the music scene. He felt that his talent would be more highly valued and music, as a profession, more accepted. He expanded his music repertoire and rediscovered the energy that he had found in playing rock and roll. He longed for the "old days" when performers were energetic on stage. "They got everybody into it," Joel remembers, "with dancing, contests, and such. They were real performers. I'm a performer. I love to perform."

Unfortunately, the drug scene took its ugly toll on this aspiring musician. An already depleted self-image was even more damaged by the debilitating effects of the drugs. The final realization that he was unable to support himself as a musician also contributed to a state of serious depression. Life was not going well at all for Joel Bonnecarre. While other men his age were making and achieving long-term goals, Joel had to give up his life-long passion to be a professional musician. He was only concerned with the fundamental human need to find food and shelter. His depression deepened. He was lost. He had dug a huge hole for himself. The light at the end of Joel's tunnel was dimming rapidly, almost ready to be extinguished.

Fortunately, his good friend, Misty, could see great value in this depressed, blind musician; value that he could not see for himself. She extended a helping hand to Joel and became an important catalyst as he looked within to find the strength to pull himself out of the deep pit he had created. "Misty really helped me out a lot, bless her heart," Joel says. "She pulled me out of the trash that I was in and showed me a different way."

Misty first recommended some ideas for making money. Because of his state of despondency, Joel was not very receptive to most of them. When she suggested he try something in the computer arena, Joel was again cool to the idea. Misty reminded him that he was very good with the electronic equipment he used on stage, but Joel really had no desire to work with a computer keyboard. Perhaps it was the fact that he only typed about eight words a minute that created the barrier in his mind. Joel knew that no one would hire a blind person for computer input of any kind who had such low numbers. Besides, he had never taken his father's advice to learn Braille when he still had some vision.

Now, faced with the prospect of never finding a quality opportunity in life, Joel started to believe what Misty was telling him. He went to Arizona Industries for the Blind and began the difficult process of learning both Braille and the computer keyboard. He raised his speed from those paltry 8 words a minute to almost 60 — and he was finally able to master Braille.

Joel learned a lot about himself during this transition from pit to potential. Hard work had never been a problem for him. He had invested an extraordinary amount of time and effort in the pursuit of his dream to become a musician. The heavy work demand required to learn essential employment skills was something he was accustomed to. It felt good to have a goal again. It was stimulating to learn and grow and reach. Maybe he really could reverse the direction of the downward spiral his life had taken. He just needed a break.

Joel had never really lost his motivation. There were many things he wanted to accomplish in life. What he had lost was his self-esteem. When a person loses a sense of worth, even simple tasks appear to be insurmountable. Thoughts of, "I can't," or "It's too hard," or "I don't deserve it" take control. Joel didn't think that he would ever amount to much because he didn't value himself. However, after working so hard to learn some fundamental skills, he serendipitously developed more self-confidence. Later, Joel realized that learning and belief in oneself almost always come as a pair, a matched set.

Armed with more confidence and a better sense of himself, Joel was prepared to enroll in the BOOST program he had learned about more than a year and a half earlier. His keyboard expertise was well beyond the minimum requirement and he was fluent in Braille, a skill he would need in order to use the Alva Braille computer terminal for his future customer service work. "I didn't think they would ever accept my blood," Joel remembers, "So I kept a band-aid on my self esteem. BOOST helped to apply the ointment to my wound that ultimately cured my disease."

Joel's mother had always taught him that humor has the seed to lighten every heavy heart. She said, "Son, you will go anywhere you want to in life if you just have a good sense of humor about things. If you don't have a good sense of humor, you will go nowhere." Joel internalized his mother's counsel, utilizing his quick wit and personality to light the path on the road to his personal renaissance. He has a widely known proclivity for teasing and poking harmless fun, especially at his himself and his blindness. Others who have endeared themselves to Joel also find themselves as the brunt of his mischief. They wear it proudly as a badge of honor.

Employed in a full-time job with a great future, married to his wonderful Teresa, and soon to be a father himself, Joel Bonnecarre now wears his own badge of honor.

We would do well, as we celebrate the refurbishing of this unusual man, to ask ourselves what we can learn from his life. Joel is the first to suggest that his life should not be considered a model, only a living reminder that the most severe obstacles can be over-come. "I've been there," Joel observes. "I've been frustrated. I've been to the point where I've cursed out every single person and then gone and medicated myself almost out of this world. OK? I almost passed away because of drugs. I've been there and I've been deep, deep down in that pit. And I can tell you you've got to get yourself back up. I guarantee that you can do it! You can do it! You can do it! I've known worse than you. I now know better than you. I can do it, you can do it!"

With such a determined perspective, Joel is abundantly pre-pared for the future. A life that was completely barren is now over-flowing with promise. His life is driven not by a world that has changed, but by a man who realized his own potential. "Sure there were small disappointments, times when I thought I would never make it, but I'm here. I am a productive man now. I didn't really ever feel very productive before. I feel like a new man!"

Tu

 · ‖ ≈ ◆ ❯❍❮ ◆ ≈ ‖ ·
---

*T*he story of Tu LePage is a kaleidoscope of human values, frailties, illness, survival, bereavement, happiness, discouragement, and, finally, the ultimate conquering of oneself and the conditions into which one is born. It is a complex assortment of surreal challenges locked in mortal combat with an improbable "glass is never empty" attitude. Tu's experience is defined by abuse and tragedy; her character by courage and optimism.

Life in French-occupied Vietnam was chaotic in the early 1950's. No centralized government framework existed to provide stability. Great uncertainty was the only constant. An open market in heroin flourished in the confusion, creating dangerous armed conflicts among drug lords relentless to expand their power base. Other more global political agendas did nothing but add to the turmoil. It was into this chaos that a beautiful baby girl named Tu was born to Chinese parents.

Tu's family was quite wealthy due to her father's involvement in the drug trade, not illegal under French law at the time. When Tu was about six years old, her parents decided to send her to live with a nun the family had earlier befriended. Her father thought that Tu might become spoiled if she stayed at home. Although she had already experienced some cultural bias against females, Tu was stunned by the physical and psychological abuse she endured for more than two years as a child servant.

Unexpectedly, an associate became disloyal to her father and the family wealth was totally depleted. No longer was it appropriate for Tu to remain with the nun, nor were her parents able to care for her. She began a process of hopping from relative-to-relative, living with aunts, uncles, and grandparents — anyone who would provide shelter and food. Tu saw her parents just once or twice a year during this time. She remembers being very lonely. "Many nights I fall asleep just missing my parents," she says. "I didn't feel abandoned but nobody can understand how a child can get away from parents. I was just missing them."

A slight turn of the kaleidoscope shows an older, unmarried sister who teaches school. Tu and her three brothers, one older and two younger, were invited to live with their sister. Another incongruity evolves with this phase of Tu's life. The sister was genuine in her desire to provide a home for her siblings, while at the same time unequipped to give the love and nurturing they so desperately needed. "She did not give me any time to do like a young child," Tu remembers. "I don't have time to talk with my friends. All of my school friends don't want to come see me. I like to go see them and I feel really jealous when they have their parents that take care of them."

Tu's sister was paid for teaching, but her limited funds were quickly drained dry by the task of providing for her siblings. Tu and her brothers were urgently required to rummage for anything they could do that would produce additional income. While still in her childhood, personal responsibility became part of Tu's fundamental character. She learned how to work hard as she searched for creative ways to make money. "When I come to this country, my friends say I work too hard," Tu says. "I tell them, 'You don't really know what hard work is.'"

An excerpt in Tu's own words helps explain some of the intimidating demands made on this 11 year-old girl and her 9 year-old brother as they carried out one of their many responsibilities. "We have to sell sandwich to go to school. Every morning we wake up about four o'clock. We have to ride bicycle maybe two miles to pick up the bread and at that time war going on. There is fighting and there is no light in the street. Some roads are paved. Some are mud and sand because a lot of roads were for wagon with cow. The wagon use that road so they make lots of ditches. It is still nighttime and we have to battle really hard to get light on bicycle because light goes on by how strong we pedal. Sometimes you stuck in the sand and you have to push, so it is hard work. And at nighttime you don't know what is going on sometimes. People fighting; we hear guns and sometimes they ask us who we are. 'We just a couple kids trying to buy some bread,' we say. It was scary and it was hard work."

A deal was worked out with the school principal so the siblings could live with Tu's sister in her little adobe house in the schoolyard. In exchange for the living arrangements, Tu and her younger brother were required to do a number of other chores in addition to the long trek in the early morning to get bread. Tu describes one of the rigorous afternoon job assignments this way, "We have to carry in the water for the school bathroom. We have no running water so we only use water from the outside well. And you know it deep well and we have to carry all the way up to the bathroom for the school. It is a lot of work every day."

While the siblings were living at the school, Tu's parents worked very hard to reconstruct their lives by building a grocery store with a small, attached restaurant. Their hard work was rewarded with financial success. "My sister decides she doesn't want me anymore, so she sends me home," Tu remembers, "not because I want to go home because I want to go to more school. She tells me, 'That's enough, parents need now so go home.'"

Increased infiltration of North Vietnamese militia into South Vietnam in the late 1960's leads to even greater confusion. "They look like the same people," Tu suggests, "so we don't know

North Vietnam from South Vietnam." These were difficult times that created immense obstacles for Tu and her family. "I was born in war time and I left in war time," Tu remembers.

The year 1969 will be permanently etched in the kaleidoscope memory tabs. Up to this point, the changing landscape of Tu's life had been evolutionary, focusing on a little girl making her way through the formative school years amid all the turmoil of expanding war. She helped rebuild her family's economic stability by working hard in the grocery store for two years, only to watch in horror as years of hard work were destroyed in an instant.

The family house did not have a back door. Shortly before a barrage of bombs and artillery shells began to drop in their village, Tu's father had a premonition. He punched a hole in the rear wall large enough for the family to escape, if necessary. The intuition proved providential when a bomb crashed through the roof and landed right in the middle of her brother's bed on the second floor. He had already been carried downstairs by his parents as the house exploded into a raging inferno. The family was able to escape from the flames through the hole in the rear wall. "The next day we come back and everything is gone," Tu painfully recalls. "All our wealth is burned to the ground. I saw people dying in the streets. Fortunately, we have no one die in our family, but it is just a scary moment in my life."

The family had lost everything for the second time. Tu's mother became very ill within a week of the destruction, the result of heartbreak from losing the family home and business. However,

Tu believes her mother's illness had much more to do with the cumulative effect of a difficult life. "In our country when you get your son married, that mean the girl owned by the husband family. She has to be a slave for her husband, her husband parents, sisters, everybody. So my mother work very hard all her life."

As had been done several times before, the family, now living in a Red Cross refugee camp, set out to rebuild their lives — and the kaleidoscope rotates to yet another panorama. Tu's mother's health continued to deteriorate. She was sent to a county hospital for prolonged treatment. Tu told her father, "I need to go out and work, do something to help my mother because I couldn't live like that. I feel really sick inside seeing my mother in the county hospital and I want to take care of her because she just lay there."

This was not the perfect time for a girl in her mid-teens to find a well-paying job that could help reverse the family misfortune. Tu made a decision to look for work in the next village, which was located near an American military base. A girlfriend introduced her to someone with a dry cleaning contract for the men on the base. Tu was hired at a very low wage to collect, count, and deliver laundry. The money scarcely covered her basic needs, let alone any surplus to help provide better medical care for her mother.

A civilian engineer from the Philippines, who had significant responsibility at the base, took an interest in the young laundry delivery girl. Tu was an attractive teenager who was desperate to find some way to help her mother. Part of her adolescent naiveté was a result of the rigid lessons she learned so painfully from the nun she had lived with earlier in her life. Tu had been force-fed a diet of complete trust through badgering and physical abuse. No middle ground existed. The nun had insisted that Tu never lie nor disobey her elders and never question anything she was told by adults. A theoretical idealism that rarely manifests itself in human reality helped to foster a natural trap for an unsuspecting and inexperienced little girl. "He find out about my situation through my boss," Tu explains in retrospect, "so he try to bait me, like fishing. He say, 'If you be my companion, I take care of your mom. I will give you money to take her to a private doctor.'" Tu loved her parents. She would have done almost anything to help her mother get the medical care she needed.

Tu was not schooled in worldly ways. Her culture was very secretive about the maturation process, hesitant to promote dialogue between parents and children regarding procreation, pregnancy, and protection. After a few short months, Tu became pregnant. "It is big disgrace in my country when the girl becomes pregnant without marriage," Tu is quick to acknowledge. "And my mother keep talking when we were young if I were ever to get pregnant without marriage, she would kill me. Put poison in my food and I would die."

Tu's life had been turned upside down. She was frightened more by the thought of her mother's response to the perceived disgrace than by the war that was raging around her. "Oh, I was scared and I go home and cry to my father," Tu explains. He was aware of the source of the extra money that Tu had provided for her mother's medical care. She had not lied to him. Her motives were pure; every dollar Tu had received went to improve her mother's chance of survival. A bizarre irony rears its head when decisions that spawn such wonderful humanity reflect so poorly on the sincere, albeit naïve, actions of a loving daughter to save her gravely ill mother.

Though her mother was struggling through a difficult, five-month hospital recuperation, Tu's father found a way to talk to his wife about Tu's pregnancy. Rather than fly into a rage, Tu's mother recognized the sacrifice that her daughter had made. "And then the man that I met," Tu shares, "after seven months, he move away and said that he would send me money to take care of my child. I never hear from him again. He did not even see the baby." With the help of a midwife, while the family was literally living in a tent on the street, Tu gave birth to a beautiful baby girl.

The kaleidoscope of Tu's life revolves to a new position, images struggling to connect in a thorny collage. A young girl is confronted with the reality of raising her baby daughter under extraordinary conditions. Another civilian appeared on the scene, this time someone with a little more integrity. Tu met him at the officers club on the American base where she was working. From the beginning, he was honest with her about his intentions. "He told me he would take care of my parents and my child for me," Tu affirms. "He just want someone to take care of him for companionship." A solution to this new wave of economic crisis was as simple as connecting the dots on a children's puzzle: provide food and clothing for her daughter in exchange for giving her exclusive affection in a new relationship. The decision was elementary; Tu became his companion.

She lived with this man while her baby daughter stayed with Tu's parents in temporary government housing. A short time passed before another series of traumatic events triggered more pain and suffering for Tu and her family. The house the family lived in was again destroyed by fire in a freak accident. "I'm lucky I didn't lose my child," Tu says. "One week after that my mom die." To add to the burden, Tu's daughter became very ill with high fever and diarrhea and her younger brother broke his leg. "I went crazy," Tu recalls. "I had to take care of my father, my boyfriend, and brother in the hospital."

While still in her teens, Tu got pregnant for the second time. Her companion was very happy with the new baby, but he and Tu never married because of some significant circumstances. First of all, he had a wife back in the United States; and second, Tu had never been in love with him. "I don't have that kind of relationship," she declares. "He took care of my father; he took care of my brother and my children, so he really good man. But I didn't love him." They stayed together for three years.

The colors of the kaleidoscope distill in a relatively pleasant array for a time, until the rings focus on the 1975 collapse of South Vietnam, a defining moment in Tu's life. Conditions were very chaotic at the end of the war, but Tu's American companion was reluctant to leave. "He did not want to go home without his child; the only child he had," Tu asserts. "But I couldn't leave my child.

I don't know how people could leave children." Tu and her companion were evacuated to the Philippines, along with her daughter and the child they had together. With all the confusion, Tu was not able to get in touch with her father before she abruptly fled Vietnam to begin a new life with her children in the United States.

Tu's companion wanted his child to be close to him, even though the homecoming included returning to a wife in Maryland. He helped Tu find a place to live in Lexington Park, where she also found a job waiting tables in a Chinese restaurant. She adjusted to life in this strange new land by working long hours and caring for her two children, now ages five and three. Her English was not very good at the time and she had little clothing. She was lonely, yet felt very fortunate that she had a fresh start. True to her character, Tu told her companion she no longer wanted his financial support. "Because I can work now, I earn my own living; I don't have to depend on him anymore. I'm happy! Finally I can make decisions for myself and my children only!"

From this exhilarating feeling of independence and opportunity has sprung a broad spectrum of conflicting images. Tu met her first husband while working in the restaurant. They were married shortly afterward and moved to Hawaii, along with her two girls. Another child, this time a boy, was born while the family lived in Hawaii. Life was good for Tu and the children! Her husband, on the other hand, was a navy pilot working a desk job and was restless. When the opportunity arose, he took a job as a civilian test pilot on the mainland, requiring a family move to California. "I knew something was in my husband that I couldn't get out of him," Tu laments. "My kids had a really good father, he's a good man. But I know something missing there; I don't know what." Unfortunately, Tu's marriage did not endure.

A rotation of the kaleidoscope reveals the young mother working as a solo act, devastating news jolting the moment: Tu's second daughter, Cathy, is diagnosed with Leukemia while just 16 years old. A bone marrow transplant was performed, causing the young teenager to slip in and out of a coma for several months. Finally, she gained permanent consciousness, left without much of what she had previously learned. "Once you get out of coma, you have to learn everything like a baby again," Tu says. "She can't communicate. They gave her an alphabet board; she blink her eyes and nurses put the word together. That how she communicate with the nurse."

After a year of therapy and concentrated care, Cathy gained enough strength to join her mother and younger brother on a trip to Lake Tahoe, California. "We have wonderful and valuable time share together," Tu explains. But the children and Tu will never forget the results of that vacation. While driving to a restaurant for breakfast before leaving Lake Tahoe, Tu suffered a massive grand mal seizure. She mumbled a response to a question from one of her children, almost hit a pedestrian, and slammed into a telephone pole head on. The car was half destroyed, but the most frightening thing for the children was watching the seizure, and its violent manifestations, take hold of their mother.

Cathy drove their partially operable car to the hospital, carefully following the ambulance in which her mother was riding. When Tu was later informed of the events, she realized the incredible feat her daughter had performed. Coupled with her weakened condition after a year of chemotherapy and coma, Cathy was considerably disabled. Still, she was able to drive the car to the hospital without further incident.

Tu had never had serious headaches or recognizable symptoms. There was no previous diagnosis of any problem. The tests, however, were indisputable: Tu had a brain tumor that needed immediate surgical removal if she were to survive. She was advised that the recovery period would require one full year with little activity. Tu's daughter, Cathy, who was making a valiant attempt to save her own life from the ravages of Leukemia, made a personal commitment that she would take care of her mother for that year.

Watching her daughter wage such a courageous struggle caused Tu a great deal of emotional pain. "Sometimes it's so hard," Tu says, recalling the tender memories. "Sometimes I wish to God if He love her just let her get well; and if He did not want, then to take her." Tu's brain surgery was performed on August 14, 1992. Cathy died on August 17, 1993 — almost exactly one year later.

Before she died, Cathy gave her mother some excellent advice. "Mom," she said, "You better go find someone else to take care of you. Nobody is going to come and knock on your door." Tu met her current husband through a friend three months before Cathy died. "My husband came into my life at the right time," Tu suggests.

"It was too much for me to take. I need him most to lean on. He was there for me. He help me to cope with the loss of my child."

During the long recovery after her brain surgery, Tu was the recipient of a wonderful ongoing act of kindness from a former real estate client. The lady had observed the struggle Cathy was having trying to prepare meals for the family. "For two months," Tu almost reverently recalls, "they bring three plates of dinner at 5:00 every night — one for me, my daughter, and son. Three dinner plates and they were just my clients. Can you believe it? How can you find people like that? Still to this day I remember that."

Tu and her husband moved from California to Ohio in response to her husband's job transfer. He was regularly out of the country on work assignments, so she made the decision to find a job. Tu worked at a restaurant and a retail store until she became very ill one day at work. A friend rushed her to the doctor where she was diagnosed with cirrhosis of the liver. Although the condition was not precipitated by alcohol consumption, doctors originally believed a liver transplant would be necessary in order to preserve Tu's life. She was referred to a liver specialist at Ohio State University, who prescribed a regimen of proper nutrition, effective medication, and substantial rest. Tu was advised to go on Social Security Disability Insurance (SSDI) during her recovery to allow time off work for the treatment protocols.

Eventually, her liver condition improved, leaving one significant postscript. Water pills that were prescribed as part of the medication seemed to be the catalyst for the development of severe osteoporosis. To this day, Tu cannot raise either arm above her shoulder.

When Tu had recovered sufficiently, she got in touch with the Ohio Bureau of Vocational Rehabilitation Services. Her counselor suggested looking into the BOOST program at Discover Card, and, as they say, the rest is history. Tu quickly became a model student and model employee, her charismatic personality being effectively utilized to encourage the most difficult customers to pay their bills. She recently received the Pinnacle of Excellence Award at Discover Card, a recognition given for superior service by senior management. It is one of the most prestigious awards the company offers.

The qualities that define Tu's character create a huge dichotomy when compared to the backdrop of her life experience. From a turbulent environment of danger, abuse, and manipulation has sprung a person of enduring energy and self-confidence.

Tu LePage is a remarkable woman. The sunlight and darkness of her life are contrasted in nouns that define her life experience as opposed to adjectives that epitomize the attributes of her character:

13

Abuse	Accountable
Brain surgery	Bright
Coma	Courageous
Death	Determined
Ex-husbands	Energetic
Fear	Family-centered
Grand mal seizure	Goal-oriented
Heartbreak	Hard-working
ICU	Inspirational
Jealousy	Jovial
Knuckleheads	Kindhearted
Leukemia	Loyal
Manipulation	Magnetic
Naiveté	Nurturing
Osteoporosis	Optimistic
Pain	Passionate
Quagmire	Quick-witted
Refugee	Resilient
Suffering	Self-reliant
Tragedy	Tenacious
Unexpected pregnancy	Unselfish
Violence	Vibrant
War	Wise
Xtreme danger	Xtremely talented
Yoke	Youthful
Zealots	Zany

But in the end, these are just words. They are used to describe the essence of this amazing woman. Tu LePage has survived war and terrible adversity to rise to a truly admirable level of personal success and professional achievement. The view through her personal kaleidoscope is refreshingly bright, rich colors blending beautifully to reflect the peace of the moment and the promise of an even better tomorrow.

Marilyn

---

ranky is a nickname normally associated with a person who is irritable, selfish, and fundamentally offensive. It is not the customary monogram attached with great affection to the female partner in a love story. But this is no ordinary woman, and this is no ordinary love story.

Clarence and Marilyn found each other the second time around. Circumstances combined to bring them together in Tempe, Arizona, where Marilyn, a single mom, was living with her three boys. She had been divorced after 11 years of marriage and earned most of her income as a landlady. Clarence was looking for a place to live. As the principle of serendipity teaches, Clarence found the comfortable apartment he was specifically seeking, along with the greater gift of his soul mate for life.

Their marriage was quite a Brady-bunch production. The family ballooned overnight to 11 with Marilyn contributing three children, Clarence doubling her with six, plus the two lovebirds that created the new nest. All of the children lived with Marilyn and Clarence, but "his" and "hers" just didn't seem to tax the full potential of the family living quarters. Two more children came from the new collaboration and the circle was finally completed with 11 children.

A union with this description is not uncommon today. Stepparents frequently raise children. They are often merged together in a pot of diversity that includes his, hers, and ours. Far less common, however, is a family amalgamation that is blended so well that labels disappear and barriers evaporate. It all seems to spring from the abiding love that is shared by two people who immensely value each other. "This gentleman (Clarence) is a great person for me," Marilyn has said so many times. "I don't know what I would do without him now."

Clarence is even more fervent in his description of their relationship. "She is the love of my life," he proudly announces with a backlog of tears welling up in his eyes. "She means so much to me. Her strength and support have helped me through so many difficult times."

Much of Marilyn's strength was undoubtedly born of her experience as a young girl. Her parents divorced and her mother died by the time she was just 11 years old. She was very aware of

"Mom's regular bouts with a rheumatic heart condition," so Marilyn was not shocked when she passed away. "It's something that you just push out of your head," she remembers. "You try not to dwell on it."

As an only child being raised by grandparents, Marilyn learned some valuable lessons about unconditional love, lessons that helped her prepare for the daunting task of raising 11 children. A self-described "typical family with typical problems" of that size would, nonetheless, severely test the patience and endurance of the best prepared among us.

Because resources were a serious challenge in the lean days as a single mom and later with her expanded family, Marilyn worked most of her adult life. She became a professional seamstress making jeans and overalls in a factory, a talent that served a multiple purpose as she helped care for her large family. Later, she went to work for a private company that owned several group homes for people with physical and psychological disabilities. Her responsibilities included preparing clients for entrance into the workforce by teaching them skills that would help them find and maintain long-term employment.

Ironically, just a few years later, Marilyn found herself being the one in need of upgrading her employable skills. An unusual problem with a dying artery in her hand caused three of her fingers to become badly discolored and, essentially, unusable. The operation that was needed to replace the artery required some time off work for recuperation. Although her employer had made assurances that her job would be available when she was able to return, they reneged on their promise. Marilyn, 55 years old with skills that were a mismatch for a high-tech world, was out of a job.

Clarence had developed a productive career for himself as a house painter in spite of the terrible disability he had lived with for more than 50 years. His knee was shattered in 1945 at the end of World War II. After 13 operations that resulted in a multitude of ugly scars and, finally, a complete fusion of the knee, Clarence was declared 40 percent disabled by the Veteran's Administration. This house painter who could not work because his knee didn't bend even one degree was judged to be less than half disabled, a distinction that netted the family only $450 a month in assistance.

Clarence waxes philosophical as he sits in his favorite chair with one leg bent naturally, foot planted firmly on the floor, the other leg jutting straight out like a steel girder hanging off the back of a flatbed truck. "We just weren't able to make ends meet with my disability assistance and her unemployment check, so my wife knew she needed to find a job pretty fast if we were going to keep our head above water."

Marilyn hit the pavement searching for something, anything, that would provide additional income as well as medical benefits that she knew would be needed in the future. "I applied for just about every job in Phoenix," Marilyn says. "The response was always the same: 'You're too old' or 'You don't have the right skills.' It was clear to me that when you're 50 years old you might as well forget it."

While she knew a woman can't do much to change her chronological age, she was also convinced that expertise could be upgraded. A semester of college to acquire some contemporary business skills resulted in another goose egg in the jobs-offered column. Months rolled by while Marilyn moved from one job interview to another, always with the same rebuff. The rejection began to transcend the monetary need and attack her self-image. She became very discouraged, which led to a dark cloud of depression.

Her spirits were raised dramatically when she was introduced to one of the BOOST program recruiters. "I remember us sitting at the table in that room talking about how everyone said I was too old, and this person said, 'No! No! No! You have a lot to contribute,'" Marilyn recalls. "They told me I just needed to learn the computer and I would be a valuable employee."

She was accepted into the program and immediately experienced a rush of adrenaline. "Of course, I was nervous and excited when I first walked into the Discover Card building," she recalls. "But I just felt comfortable with capital letters. The warm feeling you got was very special. Everyone was so helpful. People are saying hi to you like they had known you for years."

Much of the positive reaction she experienced was obviously connected to Marilyn's own ability to make people around her feel comfortable. She soon bonded with the younger "kids" who were her classmates at BOOST. They considered her to be the mother of the class. "Because I was the oldest in the class, if people had a problem or something, they would come to mom to talk about it," Marilyn explains. Many of those she helped believe that it was not her age but her patient, non-judgmental listening ear that created the magnet of attraction.

Before long, the friendships she was developing became even more important than the skills she was acquiring. The long-time barriers to learning that Marilyn honestly believed were insurmountable dissolved quickly as she absorbed the computer training like a sponge. "The difference in her outlook was amazing," Clarence remembers. "She was so happy; she talked about it every day."

Marilyn was thrilled when she graduated from BOOST and accepted a job as a customer account representative. She thought to herself, "I made it! And proved them wrong: No one is ever too old to learn new things." About a month after beginning the Discover Card training for her specific job, Marilyn's world was once again turned upside down.

Clarence had been struggling with severe internal bleeding. Varicose veins in his esophagus had produced a serious condition that required immediate surgery. He almost died during that first procedure so Marilyn took a leave of absence from her new job to nurse him back to health. "I almost lost him that first time and then I almost lost him again," she explains. "Although my job was very important to me, it was not important at all compared to getting that man back on his feet." After the second operation and, as Clarence says, "more transfusions than people have transfers on the bus," his bleeding esophagus was brought under control.

Marilyn went back to work, where she was given a hero's welcome. Kranky had returned! Her peers were excited to see their friend, confidant, counselor, and mom. You see, Marilyn had become much more than a professional associate, she was one of the family. A great kidder with a witty personality by nature, this amazing lady was also the epitome of patience, tolerance, acceptance, and unconditional love. She was outwardly focused, much more concerned with the feelings and welfare of others than her own needs. Kranky was loved by her associates for her goodness and respected by her supervisors for her high level of production and quality performance.

An air of optimism took hold in the Krankle family but was merely the calm before the storm. The traumatic events that struck with unmitigated fury during the next year jolted Marilyn and Clarence to the core. Most of us cannot begin to comprehend the emotional devastation that comes from losing a child of any age. Those who have experienced such a brutal shock almost always define it as the greatest challenge they have ever faced. Such was the case with Marilyn and Clarence when their world was rocked by the sudden death of their 42-year-old son.

Jerry lived next door with his wife and daughter. He was having problems breathing, a condition considered quite normal due to a heart murmur that had been diagnosed in his childhood, as well as a regular smoking habit. A scheduled check-up turned into a nightmare when Jerry had a heart attack during the examination. Further tests revealed some serious problems with his worn-out heart valves. Jerry was stabilized and doing quite well when he took a sudden turn for the worse. He lost consciousness. Despite heroic efforts, he was never revived.

"It's rough," Marilyn explains. "Jerry was not really my child, he was my stepson, but I raised him as my child because he wasn't that old when I got together with his father. He's always been like a son to me. I've never thought of him as my stepson. It was hard, very hard for both of us."

Jerry passed away in June. The following month Marilyn escorted Clarence to the doctor for a check-up on his breathing. While all three were sitting in the office discussing Clarence, the doctor looked at Marilyn and said, "Ma'am, how are you feeling?" She told him she was fine but that she was having a little difficulty breathing because her asthma was acting up. He said, "You need to go to the hospital." The doctor then examined her hand and said, "You're turning purple, we need to call 911."

Marilyn was rushed by ambulance to the hospital, where she was given emergency oxygen. A four-day stay ultimately produced the diagnosis of chronic obstructive pulmonary disease, a condition requiring 24-hour supplemental oxygen. Marilyn was not as concerned with the diagnosis or treatment as she was the possible effect on her job. "I love working," she says. "When they told me I had to stop because of my health, my heart was just broken."

Marilyn wanted desperately to go back to work but the doctors were concerned about a constant oxygen supply. She felt pretty good and knew she could continue to perform at the competent level she had previously achieved. A caring department manager went to bat for her and devised a way for Marilyn to get back to work. "I took my concentrator (the portable oxygen supply tank) out there, plugged it in right underneath my desk, attached the hose to my nose, and went to work," she reports.

She worked for another year with the oxygen tank as her constant companion. Kranky's arrival for her appointed shift was always punctuated by the ceremonial dragging of the portable oxygen from her parking place to the building entrance and finally to her cubicle. As the months wore on, the journey grew more and more difficult. Her health deteriorated as each breath became a courageous struggle, until the doctors finally told her it was time to leave her job. "I didn't want to quit," she says. "I came home from the doctor's office and cried forever."

Consistent with her character, Marilyn didn't complain about this final harsh twist of fate. In fact, she never complained about any of the burdens she carried, regardless of how potent their sting. She will be long remembered for the legacy of both human kindness and professional success that were permanently etched in the culture of the work she loved so much.

Several months after Marilyn made her final journey from the parking lot to her cubicle, Clarence made a phone call to inform her friends at Discover Card that his soul mate of 33 years had completed the struggle for her last breath. The love story has ended, but in a very real sense, it has just begun.

Goodbye, Kranky. Your courageous example and wonderful

influence have made an indelible impression on the lives of all you have so unselfishly touched. We will never forget you.

"Success is to be measured not so much by the
position that one has reached in life as by the obstacles
which he has overcome."

—Booker T. Washington

The Stories Continue...

L ife is a dynamic process, constantly presenting new opportunities as well as new challenges. We thought you might
be interested in this informal update on the twelve extraordinary people you have met.

DARRYL

Considers his recent heart attack a wake up call

Looks fantastic after losing a lot of weight

Continues to charm people with that wonderful voice and
demeanor

Still working at Discover Financial Services

DEBBIE

Driving for the first time in 20 years

Kids are great and she is happily married to Frank

New kidney is doing better than most original equipment

Loves her job at Discover Financial Services

DAVID

Raising three sons and expecting number four with wife Jen

Coaching his son's soccer team

Upwardly mobile career at Discover Financial Services

Loves his job as BOOST Coordinator

GINGER

Happily married to Sid

Living in Tennessee

Tumor has shrunk

She is now driving again

Susan M.

Cancer free

Happily married to Randy

Busy decorating her new home

Loves her job as BOOST Coordinator

Paul

Bought a condo

Still loves soccer

Doing volunteer work at A.I. Dupont Hospital for Children

Working in New Accounts at Discover Financial Services

Stella

Youngest son will enter BOOST in the near future

Her long-time companion recently passed away

Can no longer work

Continues her positive outlook on life

Marette

Graduated with a Masters Degree in Social Work

Active volunteer for Helping Hands in Haiti, where she has
traveled

Has become the author of several training modules

Loves her job as BOOST Coordinator

SUSAN C.

Looks terrific, has now lost 150 pounds

Enjoys breeding and raising puppies

Happily married to Bruce

Doing well in her job at Discover Financial Services

JOEL

Enjoys his young son with wife Teresa

Has two dogs

Playing bass in the rock band "Story Teller"

Still working at Discover Financial Services in Phoenix

TU

Happily married to Mel

Still living in Columbus, Ohio

Never misses a chance to help other people

Doing exceptionally well at Discover Financial Services

MARILYN

Kranky will never be forgotten!

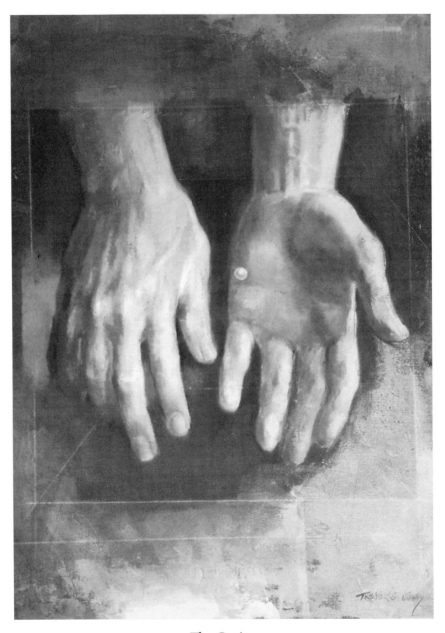

The Caring
Oil Painting by Trevor Southey

THE CARING

In my painting, *The Caring*, the pearl is a symbol of the ultimate essence of our being, our souls if you like. It is used here as a synthesis of nature and nurture with all its imperfections. Slipping from the womb, we are totally dependent, our hands probing the air in blindness. The growth to full potential rests in the hands of others and then slowly into our own. Gradually our hands become more or less capable, yet our capacity to nurture ourselves and others is limited by our individual human realities and natural limitations. That is the time when we need to be linked with those of others.

Clarity of vision is crucial for those who would respond to the needs of others. Cradling us within their care too long may suffocate our growth. Conversely cradling us too little stultifies. The art of nurture can be a wonder and a terror. Ideally, we learn from those around us all our lives, always seeking a balance so that we and those we love can reach that pearl like existence, beauty rendered most beautiful by care and the natural abrasion of living. It is an irony that often those most blessed at birth do not achieve that full beauty, while those born to woe of many kinds can rise beyond all expectations. The spontaneous compassion of our fellows is imperative.

Strange is the irony that those who respond to the woeful and lose themselves in that giving grow unconsciously more beautiful themselves. The exchange between the caregiver and the cared for, symbolized by the hands, is a means by which we can all attain a greater humanity.

— *Trevor Southey*

Artist Trevor Southey was born in Rhodesia (now Zimbabwe) in 1940. His African heritage can be traced to 17th century European colonists. In 1965, he emigrated to the United States. Southey's formal training includes stints in England and South Africa; and two degrees obtained from Brigham Young University. He taught at the University through 1977 and has since pursued his career independently. His media include drawing, printmaking, painting, stained glass, and sculpture. He has been increasingly interested in writing and has collaborated with K. Mitchell Snow of Washington D.C. in the production of a major illustrated volume about his work titled Trevor Southey: Reconciliation.

DALE INKLEY

Dale has a real passion for the people development process. For more than 30 years, he was an officer of Inkley's, a chain of retail photographic and electronics stores. He is currently president of Resource Development Systems and the author of numerous training programs. He is an active community volunteer, having served as chairman of the Utah Division of the American Cancer Society. Dale and wife, Debbie, have six children and seven grand-children.

DEBBIE INKLEY

For over two decades, Debbie Inkley has been a strong advocate for people with disabilities and a catalyst for job skills training and employment opportunities. She was the board chair of United Cerebral Palsy of Utah and the director of the Utah Governor's Committee on Employment of People with Disabilities. She is the co-founder and president of BOOST, Inc., and the founder of The Opportunity Foundation of America. Debbie lives with her husband, Dale, in Salt Lake City, Utah.

ADDITIONAL COPIES OF

DIGNITY

12 EXTRAORDINARY INDIVIDUALS
REACH FOR OPPORTUNITY

ARE AVAILABLE FROM

THE OPPORTUNITY FOUNDATION OF AMERICA

2844 East Millcreek Canyon Road
P.O. Box 9748
Salt Lake City, UT 84109 USA

Phone and Fax: 801-463-1425
Toll-Free: 800-347-7485

www.ofoa.net

$25.00 plus $2.50 shipping and handling
Major credit cards accepted

Inquire about quantity discounts for non-profits and educational groups.

Dale and Debbie Inkley continue their work on behalf of people with disabilities.
They are available for limited speaking engagements.
Please call the above number to schedule an event, or email: boostut@aol.com

For more information about BOOST, go to
www.boostinc.com